© Copyright 2018 by Jessica Zermeno - All rig

This document is geared towards providing e regards to the topic and issue covered. The publication is sold with the idea that the publisher is not required to render accounting, officially permitted, or otherwise, qualified services. If advice is necessary, legal or professional, a practiced individual in the profession should be ordered.

Legal Notice:

The book is copyright protected. This is only for personal use. You cannot amend, distribute, sell, use, quote or paraphrase any part or the content within this book without the consent of the author.

Disclaimer Notice:

Please note the information contained within this document is for educational and entertainment purposes only. Every attempt has been made to provide accurate, up to date and reliable complete information. No warranties of any kind are expressed or implied. Readers acknowledge that the author is not engaging in the rendering of legal, financial, medical or professional advice. The content of this book has been derived from various sources. Please consult a licensed professional before attempting any techniques outlined in this book.

By reading this document, the reader agrees that under no circumstances are is the author responsible for any loses, direct or indirect, which are incurred as a result the use of information contained within this document, including, but not limited to, —errors, omissions, or inaccuracies.

Table of Contents

Introduction 6

Chapter 1: Quick Guide to Whole foods 30-Program 7

    How to Do It 7

    Foods to Avoid 8

    Exceptions to The Rule 9

    How to Survive the Whole foods 30 Program 10

Chapter 2: Using the Instant Pot 11

    Instant Pot Buttons 11

    Safety Tips 12

Chapter 3: Whole foods 30 Program Approved Soup Recipes 14

        Instant Pot Beef Borscht 14

        Garden Harvest Soup 15

        Whole foods 30 Cuban Sweet Potato Soup 16

        Potato and Spinach Soup 17

        Easy Minestrone Soup 18

        Clear and Simple Beef Bone Broth 19

        Broccoli and Mushroom Soup 20

        Mexican Chicken Soup 21

        Butternut Cauliflower Soup 22

        Clear Chicken and Spinach Soup 23

        Simple Beef Soup 24

        Chunky Beef, Cabbage, and Tomato Soup 25

        Instant Pot Chicken Soup 26

        Thai Coconut Chicken Soup 27

        Thai Carrot Soup 28

        Fennel and Cauliflower Soup 29

        Fresh Kabocha Squash Chowder 30

- Whole foods 30 Italian Wedding Soup 31
- Ground Beef and Tomatoes Soup 32
- Ethiopian-Style Potato and Spinach Soup 33
- Winter Melon and Quail Eggs Soup 34
- Swiss Chard Stem Soup 35
- Whole foods 30 Goulash 36
- Simple Onion Soup 37
- Winter Spanish Soup 38

Chapter 4: Whole foods 30 Program Approved Sautéed Recipes 39

- Instant Pot BBQ Leftover Chicken 39
- Chicken and Potatoes 40
- Whole foods 30 Orange Chicken 41
- Whole foods 30 General Tso's Chicken 42
- Sautéed Rosemary Potatoes 43
- Beef and Broccoli Stir Fry 44
- Instant Pot Brussels Sprouts 45
- Whole foods 30 Cauliflower Rice 46
- Beef, Mushroom, And Zucchini Stir Fry 47
- Whole foods 30 Veggie Lo Mein 48
- Stir Fried Sesame Chicken 49
- Indian Bell Peppers and Potato Stir Fry 50
- Broccoli and Ground Beef Stir Fry 51
- Butternut Squash Stir Fry 52
- Whole foods 30 Cashew Chicken Stir Fry 53
- Sautéed Indian Butter Shrimps 54
- Chicken, Shrimps, And Okra Stir Fry 55
- Fried Japanese Cauliflower Rice 56
- Stir Fried Pork with Onions 57
- Leftover Sautéed Chicken with Applesauce 58
- Sautéed Garlic Chicken Strips 59

- Stir-Fried Garlic Shrimps 60
- Stir-Fried Vegetables 61
- Beef and Bell Pepper Stir Fry 62
- Ginger-Veggie Stir Fry 63

Chapter 5: Whole foods 30 Program Approved Casserole Recipes 64

- Potatoes and Pepper Casserole 64
- Chicken Broccoli Egg Casserole 65
- Twice Baked Potato Casserole 66
- Whole foods 30 Chicken Cordon Blue Casserole 67
- Chicken Pot Pie Casserole 68
- Whole foods 30 Chicken Enchilada Casserole 69
- Chicken Gloria Casserole 70
- Alfredo Chicken Pot Pie 71
- Creamy Mexican Casserole 72
- Sweet Potato Breakfast Casserole 73
- Spinach and Broccoli Breakfast Casserole 74
- Instant Pot Squash Casserole 75
- Beef, Mushroom, And Egg Casserole 76
- Herbed Turkey Casserole 77
- Chive and Onion Egg Casserole 78
- Mediterranean Minestrone Casserole 79
- Beef and Potato Casserole 80
- Beef and Peppers Breakfast Casserole 81
- Mixed Vegetable Casserole 82
- Extra Basil Pesto Casserole 83
- Italian Chicken and Vegetable Casserole 84
- "Baked" Fish and Veggies Casserole 85
- Shredded Turkey and Vegetables Casserole 86
- Winter Root Veggies Casserole 87
- Chicken Enchilada Casserole 88

Chapter 6: Whole foods 30 Program Approved Slow-Cooked Recipes 89

- Instant Pot Slow Cooker Turkey Chili 89
- Slow Cooker Hawaiian Kalua Pig 90
- Coconut Chicken Curry 91
- Instant Pot Applesauce 92
- Slow Cooker Shredded Chicken 93
- Slow Cooker Meatballs 94
- Slow Cooker Caramelized Onions 95
- Slow Cooker Chicken Adobo 96
- Slow Cooker Brisket and Onions 97
- Slow Cooker Pork Carnitas 98
- Coconut Curry Pork 99
- Slow Cooker Barbacoa Beef 100
- Korean Short Ribs 101
- Slow Cooker Chicken Tikka Masala 102
- Citrus-Braised Chicken in Slow Cooker 103
- Instant Pot Whole foods 30 Chili 104
- Slow Cooker Chinese Ribs 105
- Slow Cooker Beef Stew 106
- Mississippi Pot Roast 107
- Slow Cooker All-American Pot Roast 108
- Simple Short Ribs 109
- Slow Cooker Whole foods 30 Sloppy Joes 110
- Slow Cooker Lamb Leg Roast 111
- Slow Cooker BBQ Chicken Wings 112

Introduction

With obesity rates all over the world rising, it is important for people to consume healthy foods. But living a fast-paced life makes it difficult for most people to be able to have a healthy diet. In fact, most people are swayed to eating at fast-food restaurants because they don't have the time to prepare healthy meals.

Although this is the sad reality for many people, you shouldn't accept this reality as there is a way to eat healthy food without slaving all day in the kitchen. The solution is owning the Instant Pot. This book gives you everything you need to know about eating healthy and in particular, the Whole foods 30 Program. Following the Whole foods 30 Program requires you to strictly cook foods made from whole food ingredients and the task of cooking meals comes easier because of the Instant Pot.

Not only will you learn about Instant Pot and the Whole Foods 30 Program, but you will also learn how to make delicious foods so that you don't have to content yourself eating salad all day.

Enjoy!

Chapter 1: Quick Guide to Whole Foods 30 Program

It takes 30 days to push the reset button on your health so that you can change your relationship with food. This is the reason why the Whole Foods 30 Program was developed. With this method, you are encouraged to consume whole foods and avoid other ingredients such as dairy, grains, and sugar to reduce the inflammation in the body.

Following this diet is very easy. The only thing that you need to do is to focus on eating healthy whole foods for 30 days. You don't even need to count calories or purchase organic or grass-fed ingredients. But make sure that you don't cheat, skip, or give in to special occasions.

Remember that the Whole Foods 30, in a nutshell, is an elimination diet thus there are certain food and food groups that should be avoided like the plague as they cause inflammation in the body. In fact, a tiny amount of inflammatory foods introduced to the system can promote cravings, mess up the blood sugar, and affect the efficiency of the digestive system.

How to Do It

The Whole Foods 30 Program is equivalent to tough love. If you are considering this particular program to help you lose weight and improve overall health, follow the tips below on how you can successfully go through this program for a whole month.

- **Don't tell yourself that it is hard:** Just because you are not allowed to eat pizza, bacon, chips, and your other favorite junk foods, does not mean that this program is difficult. Although it may cause you a bit of discomfort when you are starting out, you need to remember you have accomplished more difficult tasks before, compared to eliminating certain foods in your diet.

- **Never slip in your diet:** Maybe you are thinking that it will not make any difference if you eat just a small bite of chocolate cake. But you are definitely wrong. A small slip can spiral your progress downwards. Be sure to stick to the program with your 100% commitment.

- **You don't have to eat anything you don't want:** We are not saying that you should start eating foods that you don't like. If you don't like a salad that is definitely Whole foods 30 compliant, then don't! The thing is that there are so many other delicious recipes that you can try without sacrificing your palate.

- **Shop and plan your meals carefully:** Being committed to this program also means that you have to shop and plan your meals carefully. It might be difficult if you have a busy time but try to sacrifice some of your time for grocery shopping. With regards to meal planning, there are so many resources that you can use to cook healthy meals.

- **Do not step on the scale:** The main idea of the Whole foods 30 Program is to make you adapt to eating healthier food choices. The focus is not on weight loss but improving your overall health. Weighing yourself daily will only make you warier about your progress while following this particular diet.

Foods to Avoid

Eating real and whole foods are the core of the Whole foods 30 Program. You can eat moderate portions of meat, eggs, and seafood but you are encouraged to consume a lot of vegetables, fruits, natural fats, herbs, spices, and natural seasonings. However, it is crucial to take note of the foods that you need to avoid while following this particular diet program.

- **Free sugar:** Free sugar refers to the type of sugar that is not naturally found in fruits. Avoid all types of free sugar–natural or artificial–and these include honey, maple syrup, agave, coconut sugar, date sugar, stevia, Nutrasweet, Equal, and so on.

- **Alcohol:** Do not consume alcohol nor use it for cooking as alcohol contains some components that can encourage inflammatory reactions in the body.

- **Grains:** Grains such as oats, rice, wheat, rye, barley, millet, sprouted grains, sorghum, quinoa, buckwheat, and amaranth.

- **Legumes:** All kinds of legumes should be avoided. This also includes legume-based products like tofu, miso, tempeh, soy milk, and many others as they contain lecithin that causes high inflammatory reactions in the body.

- **Dairy:** All forms of dairy and dairy products should be avoided as the lactose present in them can cause strain to the digestive system especially to people who suffer from lactose intolerance.

- **Baked goods:** Baked goods often contain grains, sugar, and dairy thus it is given that you should avoid consuming cakes, biscuits, pies, and all forms of conventional pastries if you are following the Whole foods 30 Program.

- **Artificial flavorings and additives:** Artificial flavorings and additives such as carrageenan, sulfites, and monosodium glutamate (MSG) should be avoided as they can also cause inflammation to occur in the body.

- **Junk foods:** Junk foods contain artificial preservatives and flavoring thus it goes against the ideals of the Whole foods 30 Program. Examples include commercially prepared potato chips, tortilla, pizza, cereals, and even ice cream.

Exceptions to The Rule

While you think that there are so many food items that you have to avoid, there are several exceptions to the rule thus allowing you to still create your favorite comfort foods while still following the diet. Below is a list of ingredients that you are allowed to use for the Whole foods 30 Program.

- **Ghee or clarified butter:** While conventional butter is not allowed, ghee can be used for the Whole foods 30 Program. The reason for this is that plain butter contains milk proteins while clarified butter has none.

- **Fruit juice:** As long as the fruit juice is freshly squeezed and not added with free sugar, then you can consume it or use it for cooking Whole foods 30-compliant meals.

- **Some legumes:** Not all legumes should be avoided like a plague. Certain legumes such as green beans, snow peas, and sugar snap peas can be used as they exist in pod form instead of the bean form.

- **Coconut aminos:** Since the Whole foods 30 Program does not allow the use of soy sauce, you can use coconut aminos as an alternative.

- **Vinegar:** All forms of vinegar can be used for the Whole foods 30 Program. These include white vinegar, wine vinegar, apple cider, rice vinegar, balsamic vinegar, and many others. However, it is important to stay away from malt vinegar because it contains gluten.

- **Salt:** Salt is one of the most widely accepted seasonings for the Whole foods 30 Program although iodized salt may contain some form of sugar in the form of Potassium iodide… not table sugar really!

The Whole foods 30 Program allows you to consume healthier foods. Make sure that you use your best judgment by taking to heart the information shared in this article. But if you are not sure if an ingredient is Whole foods 30 compliant, then follow the mantra *"When in doubt, leave it out!"*

How to Survive the Whole foods 30 Program

Eating healthy for a Whole foods 30 days can be difficult for many people. The thing is that most people experience withdrawal problems especially if they have to cut sugar and grains from their lives. But aside from being committed to this program, there are several ways for you to successful with this program. Below are practical tips on how you can see yourself through this program without experiencing a lot of problems.

- **Clean your pantry and fridge:** So that you will not be tempted to cheat, clean out your pantry and fridge from foods that are not Whole foods 30 compliant. You don't need to throw them out. You can place them in a big box and have your mom, sister or friend have it for safe keeping as you might want to use them once you are finished with the program.

- **Take time for meal preparation:** You have to be active in all the meal planning and meal preparation. The idea here is to let you get familiarized with the foods to use and avoid. But if you are going to use the Instant Pot, you can cut your time in half when it comes to preparing and cooking your meal.

- **Plan ahead if you are eating out:** There are times when we cannot avoid going out with friends and family. If you are concerned about consuming foods that are not Whole foods 30 compliant, then do your research first. Learn about the restaurant where you are going and try to find out about their menu. It can also help if you eat prior to going out so you won't be tempted to eat just about any food served in front of you.

- **Get a good Whole foods 30 book:** To prepare delicious meals that are Whole foods 30 compliant, get the right book or cookbook. Luckily, you are in the right place!

Chapter 2: Using the Instant Pot

The Instant Pot is the perfect kitchen device if you want to take on the Whole foods 30 Program as it allows you to cook different types of healthy foods even if you're a novice in the kitchen. With its intuitive user interface, the Instant Pot allows you to cook your favorite foods easily. And while the Whole Foods 30 Program restricts you from cooking with certain types of ingredients, you will still be able to whip up delicious-tasting foods with the Instant Pot.

Instant Pot Buttons

The Instant Pot is a top-of-the-line electronic pressure cooker that allows you to make different types of food imaginable. If you bought one to jumpstart your Whole foods 30 Program, then let this article serve as your guide. When cooking with Instant Pot, the first things that you need to take note of are the buttons.

- **Adjust:** This button allows you to change the temperature setting and time setting so that you can customize the way you cook your meals.

- **Slow Cook:** This button allows you to turn this device into a slow cooker, so you can leave your food cooking and have it ready by the time you come back home from work.

- **Sauté:** You can use this button to sauté or simmer your food. When using this button, make sure that the lid is open so that you can stir the ingredients while cooking. This setting is also used to thicken sauces.

- **Manual:** This button allows you to customize the cooking time and temperature of your food. This is the most widely used setting of all.

- **Yogurt:** This button allows you to turn the Instant Pot into a yogurt maker. You can make coconut or nut-based yogurt anytime of the day.

- **Timer:** This button is usually used to set how long you want your food to be cooked. You can also press this button so that you can start the Instant Pot at a later time thus allowing you to cook your meals on demand.

- **Keep Warm/Cancel:** Allows you to cancel your cooking or keep it warm until you are ready to eat.

- **Pressure:** You can set the type of pressure that you want with this button thus allowing you to cook either with low or high pressure.

- **Meat/ Stew:** This button allows you to cook different types of meats.

- **Multigrain:** Used to cook rice and different grains, this particular button is not necessary if you are following the Whole foods 30 Program.

- **Bean/Chili:** This button allows you to cook bean dishes at high temperature and pressure settings.

- **Porridge:** Same with the Rice button, it allows you to cook rice as well soups with this button.

- **Poultry:** Cook different types of poultry meat with this button.

- **Soup:** This button is great for cooking soup, stews, and chowders.

- **Steam:** Usually used with a trivet, this button allows you to make all types of steamed dishes.

Safety Tips

While the Instant Pot is very easy to operate, problems may still arise especially if you don't use it properly. Thus, below are practical safety tips so that you can maximize the use of this intuitive kitchen helper.

- **Never fry food in it:** Never use this Instant Pot to fry food as the high-temperature setting may cause the oil to burn or catch fire.

- **Don't fill it with too many ingredients:** Do not fill the Instant Pot with a lot of ingredients as it might take the device to build enough pressure to cook your food. Leave enough room for the air to move inside the pressure cooker.

- **Open the quick pressure release away from you:** When doing quick pressure release, make sure that the valve does not face in your direction otherwise the hot steam might scald your face and other body parts. If you are cooking grains, which is unlikely if you are in a Whole foods 30 Program, make sure that you don't opt for this type of pressure release so that the vent will not get filled with foam that is hard to clean.

- **Clean after every use:** When cleaning the Instant Pot, pay extra attention to the lid particularly the vent and make sure that you remove the particles that clogged up the vents.

Chapter 3: Whole foods 30 Program Approved Soup Recipes

Instant Pot Beef Borscht

Serves: 6
Preparation Time: 5 minutes
Cooking Time: 45 minutes

Ingredients
- 3 beets, peeled and diced
- 3 stalks of celery, diced
- 2 carrots, peeled and diced
- 2 cloves of garlic, minced
- 1 onion, diced
- 3 cups shredded cabbage
- 6 cups water
- 1 bay leaf
- Salt and pepper to taste
- ½ cup coconut cream
- 1 tablespoon lemon juice

Instructions
1. Place all ingredients in the Instant Pot except for the coconut cream and lemon juice.
2. Give a good stir.
3. Close the lid and make sure that the vent is sealed.
4. Press the Soup button and adjust the cooking time to 40 minutes
5. Do a natural pressure release to open the lid.
6. Once the lid is open, stir in the coconut cream and lemon juice.
7. Press the Sauté button and continue stirring for 5 minutes.
8. Serve warm.

Nutrition information: Calories per serving: 120; Carbohydrates:13.7 g; Protein: 2.6g; Fat:7.8 g; Fiber: 3.7g

Garden Harvest Soup

Serves: 6
Preparation Time: 5 minutes
Cooking Time: 1 hour and 10 minutes

Ingredients
- 6 cups water
- 1-pound beef bone
- Salt and pepper to taste
- 6 cloves of garlic, minced
- 2 carrots, chopped coarsely
- 1 cup celery, chopped
- ½ cup tomatoes, chopped
- A handful of oregano
- A handful of basil
- A handful of parsley

Instructions
1. Pour in the water and add the beef bone to the Instant Pot.
2. Close the lid and make sure that the vent is sealed.
3. Press the Manual button and adjust the cooking time to 1 hour.
4. Do natural pressure release and open the lid.
5. Take out the beef bones and discard.
6. Add in the vegetables and herbs.
7. Season with salt and pepper to taste.
8. Close the lid and seal off the vent.
9. Press the Soup button and adjust the cooking time to 10 minutes.
10. Do natural pressure release.

Nutrition information: Calories per serving: 121; Carbohydrates: 4.6g; Protein: 1.8g; Fat:10.1g; Fiber: 1.2g

Whole foods 30 Cuban Sweet Potato Soup

Serves: 6
Preparation Time: 5 minutes
Cooking Time: 15 minutes

Ingredients

- 2 tablespoons extra virgin olive oil
- 1 onion, chopped
- 5 cloves of garlic, minced
- 1-pound sweet potatoes, peeled and diced
- 1 red bell pepper, chopped
- 1 cup tomatoes
- 1 bay leaf
- 1 teaspoon ground cumin
- 2 teaspoons dried oregano
- Salt and pepper to taste
- 4 cups water

Instructions

1. Press the Sauté button on the Instant Pot and stir in the onions and garlic until fragrant.
2. Add the rest of the ingredients and keep on stirring until well combined.
3. Close the lid and make sure that the vent is sealed off.
4. Press the Manual button and adjust the cooking time to 20 minutes.
5. Do natural pressure release.
6. Serve with chopped scallions or cilantro if desired.

Nutrition information: Calories per serving: 338; Carbohydrates: 52g; Protein: 17g; Fat: 5g; Fiber: 12g

Potato and Spinach Soup

Serves: 4
Preparation Time: 5 minutes
Cooking Time: 1 hour

Ingredients

- 6 cups water
- 1-pound chicken bones
- 2 tablespoons ghee
- 1 onion, chopped
- 5 cloves of garlic, minced
- 3 carrots, chopped
- ½ cup celery, chopped
- 4 large potatoes, peeled chopped
- 1 cup spinach leaves, chopped
- Salt and pepper to taste

Instructions

1. Place inside the Instant Pot water and chicken. Close the lid and seal off the vent.
2. Press the Manual button and adjust the cooking time to 40 minutes.
3. Do natural pressure release and drain the broth from the Instant Pot. Discard the chicken bones then set aside. This will be the chicken broth.
4. Press the Sauté button on the Instant Pot and melt the ghee. Stir in the onions and garlic until fragrant.
5. Add the rest of the ingredients and season with salt and pepper to taste.
6. Pour in the chicken broth.
7. Close the lid and seal off the vent.
8. Press the Manual button and adjust the cooking time to 20 minutes.
9. Do natural pressure release.

Nutrition information: Calories per serving:525; Carbohydrates: 75.4g; Protein:33.2 g; Fat: 10.8g; Fiber:11.4g

Easy Minestrone Soup

Serves: 6
Preparation Time: 5 minutes
Cooking Time: 1 hour and 3 minutes

Ingredients
- 6 cups water
- 1-pound beef bones
- Salt and pepper to taste
- 2 tablespoons olive oil
- 1 onion, diced
- 3 cloves of garlic, minced
- 2 stalks of celery, minced
- 1 carrot, diced
- 1 zucchini, diced
- 1 cup roma tomatoes, diced
- 1 cup basil leaves
- 1 teaspoon dried oregano
- 1 teaspoon dried basil
- 1 bay leaf
- ½ cup spinach, shredded

Instructions
1. Place water and beef bones in the Instant Pot. Season with salt and pepper to taste.
2. Close the lid and press the Manual button. Adjust the cooking time to 45 minutes.
3. Strain the broth and discard the bone.
4. Press the Sauté button and heat the oil. Sauté the onion and garlic until fragrant.
5. Add the rest of the ingredients except for the spinach. Pour in the bone broth.
6. Close the lid and seal off the vent.
7. Press the Soup button and adjust the cooking time to 15 minutes.
8. Do natural pressure release.
9. Once the lid is off, press the Sauté button and stir in the spinach. Cook for another 3 minutes.

Nutrition information: Calories per serving: 224; Carbohydrates: 5.4g; Protein: 22.3g; Fat: 12.7g; Fiber:1.3g

Clear and Simple Beef Bone Broth

Serves: 6
Preparation Time: 5 minutes
Cooking Time: 1 hour and 30 minutes

Ingredients
- 8 cups water
- 4 pounds of beef bones
- 2 medium carrots, sliced thickly
- 1 onion, quartered
- 1 garlic head, crushed
- 2 celery stalks, sliced
- 2 bay leaves
- 1 bunch rosemary
- 2 tablespoon black peppercorns
- Salt and pepper to taste

Instructions
1. Place all ingredients in the Instant Pot.
2. Close the lid and seal off the vents.
3. Press the Manual button and adjust the cooking time to 1 hour and 30 minutes.
4. Do natural pressure release.
5. Strain the solids or serve it as it is.

Nutrition information: Calories per serving: 154; Carbohydrates: 3.4g; Protein: 8.5g; Fat: 5.2g; Fiber: 1.6g

Broccoli and Mushroom Soup

Serves: 8
Preparation Time: 5 minutes
Cooking Time: 15 minutes

Ingredients
- 1 tablespoon ghee
- 1 onion, diced
- 3 cloves of garlic, diced
- 2 cups mushrooms, chopped
- 4 cups water
- 2 heads of broccoli, cut into florets
- Salt and pepper to taste

Instructions
1. Press the Sauté button on the Instant Pot.
2. Heat the ghee and sauté the onion and garlic until fragrant.
3. Add the mushrooms and sauté for two more minutes.
4. Add the rest of the ingredients.
5. Close the lid and press the Soup button.
6. Adjust the cooking time to 10 minutes.
7. Do natural pressure release.

Nutrition information: Calories per serving: 31; Carbohydrates: 3.11g; Protein: 1.2g; Fat: 1.9g; Fiber: 0.7g

Mexican Chicken Soup

Serves: 4
Preparation Time: 5 minutes
Cooking Time: 20 minutes

Ingredients
- 3 chicken breasts, bones removed and chopped
- 2 teaspoons chili powder
- 2 teaspoons ground cumin
- 1 cup tomatoes, chopped
- 5 cups water
- 1 cup zucchini, chopped
- 1 tablespoon lime juice
- Salt and pepper to taste

Instructions
1. Place all ingredients in the Instant Pot.
2. Close the lid and seal off the vents.
3. Press the Manual button and adjust the cooking time to 20 minutes.
4. Do natural pressure release.

Nutrition information: Calories per serving: 395; Carbohydrates: 4.1g; Protein: 46.3g; Fat: 20.7g; Fiber: 1.2g

Butternut Cauliflower Soup

Serves: 6
Preparation Time: 5 minutes
Cooking Time: 15 minutes

Ingredients

- 1 teaspoon extra virgin olive oil
- 1 onion, diced
- 3 cloves of garlic, chopped
- 1 head cauliflower, cut into florets
- 1 large butternut squash
- 6 cups water
- 1 teaspoon paprika
- ½ teaspoon thyme
- ¼ teaspoon red pepper flakes
- Salt and pepper to taste
- 1 cup coconut milk, freshly squeezed

Instructions

1. Press the Sauté button on the Instant Pot.
2. Heat the oil and sauté the onion and garlic until fragrant.
3. Add the rest of the ingredients except for the coconut milk.
4. Close the lid and sea off the vent.
5. Press the Manual button and cook for 10 minutes.
6. Do natural pressure release.
7. Once the lid is open, press the Sauté button and Add the coconut milk.
8. Simmer for 5 minutes.

Nutrition information: Calories per serving: 133; Carbohydrates: 9.5g; Protein: 2.9g; Fat: 10.6g; Fiber: 3g

Clear Chicken and Spinach Soup

Serves: 6
Preparation Time: 5 minutes
Cooking Time: 20 minutes

Ingredients
- 2-pound chicken breasts, cut into chunks
- 6 cups of water
- 3 cloves of garlic, crushed
- 1 onion, quartered
- 1 thumb-size ginger, sliced
- ½ cup tomatoes, chopped
- Salt and pepper to taste
- 2 cups spinach, shredded

Instructions
1. Place all ingredients in the Instant Pot except for the spinach.
2. Close the lid and seal off the vents.
3. Press the Manual button and adjust the cooking time to 20 minutes.
4. Do natural pressure release.
5. Once the lid is open, press the Sauté button and Add the spinach.
6. Allow to simmer for 5 minutes.

Nutrition information: Calories per serving: 277; Carbohydrates: 3.8g; Protein: 32.7g; Fat: 14.1g; Fiber: 0.8g

Simple Beef Soup

Serves: 6
Preparation Time: 5 minutes
Cooking Time: 1 hour and 5 minutes

Ingredients
- 1 ½ pounds stew meat, cut into chunks
- Salt and pepper to taste
- 2 tablespoons olive oil
- 10 baby Bella mushrooms, chopped
- 8 cloves of garlic, minced
- 1 onion, chopped
- 1 stalk of celery, chopped
- 1 carrot, chopped
- 7 cups water
- 2 bay leaves
- ½ teaspoon thyme
- 1 large potato, grated

Instructions
1. Season the beef stew with salt and pepper to taste.
2. Press the Sauté button on the Instant Pot and heat the oil.
3. Sear the beef on all sides for at least 5 minutes.
4. Stir in the mushrooms, garlic, onion, and celery until fragrant.
5. Add the rest of the ingredients.
6. Stir to combine and remove the browning on the bottom of the pot.
7. Close the lid and seal off the vent.
8. Press the Meat Button and adjust the cooking time to 1 hour.
9. Do natural pressure release.

Nutrition information: Calories per serving: 418; Carbohydrates:20.1g; Protein: 34.4g; Fat: 22g; Fiber: 2.9g

Chunky Beef, Cabbage, and Tomato Soup

Serves: 7
Preparation Time: 5 minutes
Cooking Time: 20 minutes

Ingredients
- 1-pound lean ground beef
- Salt and pepper to taste
- ½ cup diced onions
- ½ cup diced celery
- ½ cup diced carrot
- 1 cup tomatoes, chopped
- 5 cups shredded cabbages
- 5 cups water
- 1 bay leaf

Instructions
1. Press the Sauté button on the Instant Pot and place the ground beef.
2. Season with salt and pepper to taste. Stir and Add the onions and celery until fragrant.
3. Place all ingredients in the Instant Pot.
4. Close the lid and seal off the vents.
5. Press the Manual button and adjust the cooking time to 20 minutes.
6. Do natural pressure release.

Nutrition information: Calories per serving: 181 Carbohydrates: 14g; Protein: 15.5g; Fat: 6g; Fiber: 2g

Instant Pot Chicken Soup

Serves: 6
Preparation Time: 5 minutes
Cooking Time: 20 minutes

Ingredients
- 2 pounds of chicken meat, sliced into bite-sized pieces
- 2 carrots, chopped
- 1 stalk of celery, chopped
- 3 cloves of garlic, minced
- 1 onion, chopped
- 6 cups water
- 1 radish, cubed
- 1 teaspoon parsley
- 1 teaspoon thyme
- 1 bay leaf
- Salt and pepper to taste

Instructions
1. Place all ingredients in the Instant Pot.
2. Close the lid and seal off the vents.
3. Press the Manual button and adjust the cooking time to 20 minutes.
4. Do natural pressure release.

Nutrition information: Calories per serving: 269; Carbohydrates: 7.3g; Protein: 30.8g; Fat: 12.4g; Fiber:2g

Thai Coconut Chicken Soup

Serves: 4
Preparation Time: 5 minutes
Cooking Time: 20 minutes

Ingredients
- 2 cups coconut milk, freshly squeezed or Whole foods 30 compliant
- 1 cup water
- 1 thumb-size fresh ginger, sliced
- 1 stalk fresh lemongrass, cut into 1-inch thick
- 1-pound chicken breasts, cut into chunks
- 1 cup sliced mushrooms
- 1 tablespoon fresh lime juice
- 2 small Thai chilies, chopped
- ¼ cup basil leaves
- ¼ cup fresh cilantro, minced
- Salt and pepper to taste

Instructions
1. Place all ingredients in the Instant Pot.
2. Close the lid and seal off the vents.
3. Press the Manual button and adjust the cooking time to 20 minutes.
4. Do natural pressure release.

Nutrition information: Calories per serving: 477; Carbohydrates: 8.2g; Protein: 26.7 g; Fat: 39.4g; Fiber: 3.9g

Thai Carrot Soup

Serves: 6
Preparation Time: 5 minutes
Cooking Time: 15 minutes

Ingredients

- 1 tablespoon olive oil
- 2 teaspoons grated ginger
- 1 onion, chopped
- 1 ¼ pound carrot, chopped
- 1 jalapeno pepper, seeded and chopped
- 4 cups water
- Salt and pepper to taste
- ½ teaspoon curry powder
- ¼ teaspoon garam masala
- ¼ teaspoon turmeric
- ¼ teaspoon cayenne pepper
- ½ cup coconut milk, freshly squeezed or Whole foods 30 compliant

Instructions

1. Press the Sauté button and heat the oil. Sauté the ginger and onion until fragrant.
2. Add the rest of the ingredient.
3. Close the lid and seal off the vent.
4. Press the Manual button and adjust the cooking time to 15 minutes.
5. Do natural pressure release.
6. Place the contents in the blender and pulse until smooth.

Nutrition information: Calories per serving: 112; Carbohydrates:11.8g; Protein: 1.6g; Fat: 7.8g; Fiber: 3.9g

Fennel and Cauliflower Soup

Serves: 4
Preparation Time: 5 minutes
Cooking Time: 15 minutes

Ingredients
- 1 tablespoon olive oil
- 1 white onion, sliced
- 3 cloves of garlic, minced
- 2 medium-sized fennel bulbs, sliced
- 1-pound cauliflower, cut into florets
- 1 cup coconut milk, freshly squeezed or Whole foods 30 compliant
- 3 cups water
- Salt and pepper to taste

Instructions
1. Press the Sauté button and heat the oil. Sauté the onion, garlic, and fennel until fragrant.
2. Stir in the rest of the rest of the ingredients.
3. Close the lid and seal off the vent.
4. Press the Soup button and adjust the cooking time to 15 minutes.
5. Do natural pressure release.

Nutrition information: Calories per serving: 240; Carbohydrates: 19.2g; Protein: 5.3g; Fat: 18.2g; Fiber: 7.4g

Fresh Kabocha Squash Chowder

Serves: 8
Preparation Time: 5 minutes
Cooking Time: 15 minutes

Ingredients
- 4 tablespoons ghee
- ½ cup onion, chopped
- 2 medium potatoes, grated
- 2 medium-sized kabocha squash, seeded and chopped
- 2 cups water
- 1 cup coconut milk, freshly squeezed or Whole foods 30 compliant
- Salt and pepper to taste

Instructions
1. Press the Sauté button and heat the ghee.
2. Sauté the onion until fragrant.
3. Stir in the potatoes and kabocha squash
4. Add the rest of the ingredients and season with salt and pepper to taste.
5. Close the lid and seal off the vent.
6. Press the Manual button and adjust the cooking time to 15 minutes.
7. Do a natural pressure release to open the lid.
8. Once the lid is open, pour the contents into a blender and pulse until smooth.

Nutrition information: Calories per serving: 213; Carbohydrates: 20.6g; Protein: 3.3g; Fat: 14.4g; Fiber: 3.4g

Whole foods 30 Italian Wedding Soup

Serves: 9
Preparation Time: 5 minutes
Cooking Time: 20 minutes

Ingredients
- ½ pounds ground beef
- 4 pounds of whole chicken, sliced into bite-sized pieces
- 1 cup sliced carrots
- 1 head escarole or cabbage, shredded
- 1 cup tomatoes, chopped
- 2 celery stalks, chopped
- 3 large potatoes, peeled and chopped
- 6 cups water

Instructions
1. Press the Sauté button on the Instant Pot and Add the ground beef.
2. Stir until the meat has rendered its fat.
3. Add the chicken slices and stir until lightly golden.
4. Add the rest of the ingredients.
5. Give a good stir to remove the browning at the bottom of the pot.
6. Close the lid and seal off the vent.
7. Press the Meat button and adjust the cooking time to 15 minutes.
8. Do natural pressure release.

Nutrition information: Calories per serving: 593; Carbohydrates: 66.5g; Protein: 42.7g; Fat: 18.4g; Fiber: 10.3g

Ground Beef and Tomatoes Soup

Serves: 6
Preparation Time: 5 minutes
Cooking Time: 20 minutes

Ingredients
- 1 teaspoon olive oil
- 1-pound lean ground beef
- 1 onion, chopped
- 1 tablespoon minced garlic
- 1 teaspoon dried thyme
- 1 teaspoon dried oregano
- 1 ½ cups tomatoes, chopped
- 6 cups water
- Salt and pepper to taste

Instructions
1. Press the Sauté button on the Instant Pot and heat the oil.
2. Add the ground beef and stir until lightly brown. Stir in the onion, garlic, thyme, and oregano until fragrant.
3. Pour in the rest of the ingredients.
4. Close the lid and seal off the vent.
5. Press the Manual button and adjust the cooking time to 20 minutes.
6. Do natural pressure release.

Nutrition information: Calories per serving: 188; Carbohydrates: 4.5g; Protein: 20.9g; Fat: 9.3g; Fiber: 1g

Ethiopian-Style Potato and Spinach Soup

Serves: 4
Preparation Time: 5 minutes
Cooking Time: 20 minutes

Ingredients

- 2 tablespoons oil
- 1 onion, chopped
- 1 teaspoon garlic powder
- 2 teaspoon ground coriander
- ½ teaspoon cinnamon powder
- ½ teaspoon turmeric powder
- ¼ teaspoon clove powder
- ¼ teaspoon cayenne pepper
- ¼ teaspoon cardamom powder
- ¼ teaspoon grated nutmeg
- 2 cups potatoes, chopped
- 8 cups water
- Salt and pepper to taste
- 2 cups spinach, chopped

Instructions

1. Press the Sauté button on the Instant Pot. Heat the oil and sauté the onion until fragrant.
2. Add the spices and fry until fragrant.
3. Stir in the potatoes and allow to fry for 3 minutes.
4. Pour in the water and season with salt and pepper to taste.
5. Close the lid and seal off the vent.
6. Press the Soup button and adjust the cooking time for 15 minutes.
7. Do natural pressure release.
8. Once the lid is open, press the Sauté button and Add the spinach. Allow to simmer for at least 5 minutes.

Nutrition information: Calories per serving: 143; Carbohydrates: 18.7g; Protein: 2.7g; Fat: 7.1g; Fiber: 3.1g

Winter Melon and Quail Eggs Soup

Serves: 6
Preparation Time: 5 minutes
Cooking Time: 1 hour and 15 minutes

Ingredients

- 1-pound pork bones
- 5 cups water
- 1 tablespoon olive oil
- 4 cloves of garlic, minced
- 1 onion, chopped
- 1 winter melon, peeled and sliced
- 10 quail eggs, pre-boiled and peeled
- Salt and pepper to taste
- Chopped cilantro for garnish

Instructions

1. Place the pork bones and water in the Instant Pot.
2. Close the lid and seal off the vent. Press the Manual button and adjust the cooking time to 1 hour.
3. Do a natural pressure release to open the lid. Remove the pork bones and set aside the broth.
4. Press the Sauté button on the Instant Pot and heat the oil.
5. Sauté the garlic and onion until fragrant.
6. Stir in the winter melon and quail eggs.
7. Season with salt and pepper to taste.
8. Pour in the broth.
9. Close the lid and press the Soup button. Adjust the cooking time to 10 minutes.
10. Do natural pressure release and garnish with cilantro.

Nutrition information: Calories per serving: 270; Carbohydrates: 9.2g; Protein: 21.9g; Fat: 16.4g; Fiber: 2.1g

Swiss Chard Stem Soup

Serves: 8
Preparation Time: 5 minutes
Cooking Time: 10 minutes

Ingredients
- 6 cups *Clear and Simple Beef Bone Broth* (recipe on page 12)
- (see recipe in this book)
- 8 cups Swiss Chard stems, diced
- 3 leeks, diced
- 1 potato, peeled and chopped
- 1 cup coconut milk
- Salt and pepper to taste

Instructions
1. Place all ingredients in the Instant Pot.
2. Close the lid and seal off the vent.
3. Press the Soup button and adjust the cooking time to 10 minutes.
4. Do natural pressure release.

Nutrition information: Calories per serving: 142; Carbohydrates: 18.3g; Protein: 3.1g; Fat: 7.4g; Fiber: 3g

Whole foods 30 Goulash

Serves: 6
Preparation Time: 5 minutes
Cooking Time: 20 minutes

Ingredients

- 2 tablespoons olive oil
- 1-pound lean ground beef
- 1 onion, chopped
- 2 cloves of garlic, minced
- 2 carrots, chopped
- Salt and pepper to taste
- 3 cups water
- 1 cup diced tomatoes
- ½ teaspoon dried thyme
- ½ teaspoon oregano
- 1 zucchini, chopped

Instructions

1. Press the Sauté button and heat the oil.
2. Add the ground beef, onion, and garlic. Continue stirring until the beef turns lightly golden
3. Stir in the rest of the ingredients.
4. Close the lid and seal off the vent.
5. Press the Manual button and adjust the cooking time to 15 minutes.
6. Do natural pressure release.

Nutrition information: Calories per serving: 227; Carbohydrates: 5.8g; Protein: 21g; Fat: 13.4; Fiber:1.4g

Simple Onion Soup

Serves: 5
Preparation Time: 5 minutes
Cooking Time: 15 minutes

Ingredients
- 2 tablespoons olive oil
- 4 large onions, sliced
- 2 bay leaves
- 5 cups *Clear and Simple Beef Bone Broth* (recipe on page 12)
- 1 teaspoon dried thyme
- Salt and pepper to taste

Instructions
1. Press the Sauté button on the Instant Pot and heat the oil.
2. Add the onions and continue stirring for 10 minutes until the onions have turned slightly caramelized.
3. Add the rest of the ingredients.
4. Close the lid and seal off the vent.
5. Press the Soup button and adjust the cooking time to 5 minutes.
6. Do natural pressure release.

Nutrition information: Calories per serving:131; Carbohydrates: 14.9g; Protein: 6.3g; Fat: 5.8g; Fiber: 2.2

Winter Spanish Soup

Serves: 5
Preparation Time: 5 minutes
Cooking Time: 35 minutes

Ingredients

- 1 ½ pounds beef stew meat, cubed
- ¼ pound chicken breasts, chopped
- 1 daikon radish, peeled and cubed
- 1 turnip, peeled and cubed
- 2 carrots, peeled and cubed
- 2 stalks of celery, chopped
- A pinch of saffron
- 6 cups water
- 1 bay leaf
- Salt and pepper to taste

Instructions

1. Press the Sauté button on the Instant Pot and Add the beef cubes and chicken breasts.
2. Stir to combine until the meats have turned lightly browned
3. Stir in the rest of the ingredients.
4. Close the lid and seal off the vent.
5. Press the Manual button and adjust the cooking time to 30 minutes.
6. Do natural pressure release.

Nutrition information: Calories per serving: 189; Carbohydrates: 9.6g; Protein: 6.9g; Fat: 13.8g; Fiber: 3.6g

Chapter 4: Whole foods 30 Program Approved Sautéed Recipes

Instant Pot BBQ Leftover Chicken

Serves: 3
Preparation Time: 10 minutes
Cooking Time: 10 minutes

Ingredients
- 5 Medjool dates, pitted
- ¼ cup organic tomato paste
- ½ cup organic applesauce (unsweetened)
- 1 teaspoon onion powder
- ½ teaspoon garlic powder
- 1 teaspoon paprika
- ½ teaspoon salt
- ¼ teaspoon black pepper
- 1 tablespoon olive oil
- 2 cloves of garlic, minced
- 2 pounds of leftover chicken, cut into shreds

Instructions
1. In a blender, combine the dates, tomato paste, unsweetened apple sauce, onion, powder, garlic powder, paprika, salt and pepper. Blend until smooth. Set aside.
2. Press the Sauté button on the Instant Pot and heat the olive oil.
3. Sauté the garlic until fragrant.
4. Add the chicken strips and pour over the barbecue sauce.
5. Stir to combine and allow to simmer for 10 minutes.
6. Serve warm.

Nutrition information: Calories per serving: 438; Carbohydrates: 16.9g; Protein: 62.8g; Fat:12.9 g; Fiber: 2.1g

Chicken and Potatoes

Serves: 6
Preparation Time: 30 minutes
Cooking Time: 15 minutes

Ingredients

- ¼ teaspoon onion powder
- ¼ teaspoon ground black pepper
- ½ teaspoon garlic powder
- ½ teaspoon salt
- ½ teaspoon paprika
- 6 chicken thighs, bones and skin not removed
- 2 tablespoons olive oil
- 3 large red potatoes, scrubbed and halved
- 1 small sprig of rosemary
- 5 tablespoons water

Instructions

1. In a mixing bowl, combine the first 5 ingredients (spices). This will be the spice rub.
2. Put the chicken in a Ziploc bag and Add the spice rub. Mix until the chicken is coated with the mixture. Place in the fridge and allow to marinate for at least 30 minutes.
3. Press the Sauté button on the Instant Pot.
4. Heat the oil and Add the chicken. Allow to sauté for at least 6 minutes and make sure that the sides turn slightly brown.
5. Add the red potatoes and rosemary and continue sautéing for another 4 minutes.
6. Stir in the water.
7. Close the lid and seal off the vent.
8. Press the Poultry button and adjust the cooking time to 10 minutes.
9. Do quick pressure release.
10. Once the lid is open, press the Sauté button again and continue stirring until the sauce has reduced, if any.

Nutrition information: Calories per serving: 598; Carbohydrates: 30.4g; Protein: 35.9g; Fat: 36.7g; Fiber: 3.3g

Whole foods 30 Orange Chicken

Serves: 6
Preparation Time: 5 minutes
Cooking Time: 15 minutes

Ingredients
- 2 tablespoons olive oil
- 5 cloves of garlic, minced
- 2 pounds of chicken breasts, cut into 1-inch pieces
- 1 cup orange juice, freshly squeezed from 1 or 2 orange fruits
- 1 tablespoon orange zest, grated
- 2 tablespoons of organic tomato paste
- Salt and pepper to taste

Instructions
1. Press the Sauté button on the Instant Pot and heat the oil.
2. Sauté the garlic until fragrant and Add the chicken breasts. Continue stirring for another 3 minutes.
3. Pour in the rest of the ingredients. Give a good stir.
4. Close the lid and seal off the vent.
5. Press the Poultry button and adjust the cooking time to 10 minutes.
6. Do quick pressure release.
7. Once the lid is open, press the Sauté button and allow the sauce to simmer until the sauce slightly thickens.

Nutrition information: Calories per serving: 343; Carbohydrates: 31g; Protein: 34g; Fat: 8g; Fiber: 4g

Whole foods 30 General Tso's Chicken

Serves: 6
Preparation Time: 5 minutes
Cooking Time: 15 minutes

Ingredients
- 1 tablespoon olive oil
- 1 onion, chopped
- 2 cloves of garlic, minced
- 2 pounds of boneless chicken breasts, sliced into thick strips
- Salt and pepper to taste
- ½ cup water
- 3 tablespoons coconut aminos
- 2 tablespoons lemon juice
- 2 tablespoons Medjool date paste (made from 5 pitted dates)
- ½ teaspoon red chili flakes
- ½ cup toasted cashew nuts

Instructions
1. Press the Sauté button on the Instant Pot and heat the oil.
2. Sauté the onion and garlic until fragrant.
3. Add the chicken breast and season with salt and pepper to taste.
4. Continue stirring for 5 minutes.
5. Stir in the water, coconut aminos, lemon juice, date paste, and red chili flakes.
6. Stir to combine.
7. Close the lid and seal off the vent.
8. Press the Poultry button and adjust the cooking time to 10 minutes.
9. Do natural pressure release.
10. Garnish with cashew nuts on top.

Nutrition information: Calories per serving: 282; Carbohydrates: 7g; Protein: 36.6g; Fat: 11.8g; Fiber: 1g

Sautéed Rosemary Potatoes

Serves: 4
Preparation Time: 5 minutes
Cooking Time: 15 minutes

Ingredients

- 2 tablespoons olive oil
- 8 large Russet potatoes, scrubbed and quartered
- 1 teaspoon salt
- ¼ teaspoon black pepper
- 1 teaspoon rosemary
- 5 tablespoons water

Instructions

1. Press the Sauté button on the Instant Pot and heat the oil.
2. Stir in the potatoes and season with salt, pepper, and rosemary.
3. Continue stirring until the potatoes edges turn slightly golden.
4. Pour in the water.
5. Close the lid and adjust the cooking time to 10 minutes.
6. Do quick natural pressure release.

Nutrition information: Calories per serving: 643; Carbohydrates: 133.5g; Protein: 15.8g; Fat: 7.3g; Fiber: 9.7g

Beef and Broccoli Stir Fry

Serves: 4
Preparation Time: 5 minutes
Cooking Time: 15 minutes

Ingredients

- 1 tablespoon peanut oil
- 3 cloves of garlic, minced
- 1 white onion, sliced
- 1-pound flank steak, sliced thinly
- ½ teaspoon five spice powder
- 1 tablespoon salt
- ½ teaspoon ground black pepper
- 2 tablespoons coconut aminos
- 7 tablespoons water
- 1 head broccoli, cut into florets

Instructions

1. Press the Sauté button on the Instant Pot and heat the peanut oil.
2. Sauté the garlic and onion until fragrant.
3. Stir in the steak and Add the five-spice powder.
4. Season with salt, black pepper, and coconut aminos.
5. Stir for at least 2 minutes.
6. Pour in water.
7. Close the lid and seal off the vent.
8. Press the Meat button and adjust the cooking time to 8 minutes.
9. Do natural pressure release.
10. Once the lid is open, press the Sauté button and Add the broccoli.
11. Allow to simmer for another 5 minutes.

Nutrition information: Calories per serving: 193; Carbohydrates: 1.7g; Protein: 24.6g; Fat: 9.1g; Fiber: 0.3g

Instant Pot Brussels Sprouts

Serves: 6
Preparation Time: 5 minutes
Cooking Time: 7 minutes

Ingredients

- 2 tablespoons sesame oil
- 2 pounds Brussels sprouts, halved
- 1 tablespoon chopped almonds
- 1 teaspoon red pepper flakes
- 2 teaspoon garlic powder
- 1 teaspoon onion powder
- Salt and pepper to taste
- 1 tablespoon coconut aminos
- 1 tablespoon lemon juice

Instructions

1. Press the Sauté button on the Instant Pot and heat the sesame oil.
2. Stir in the Brussels sprouts, almonds, red pepper flakes, garlic powder, and onion powder.
3. Season with salt and pepper to taste.
4. Add the coconut aminos and lemon juice.
5. Close the lid and seal off the vent.
6. Press the Manual button and adjust the cooking time to 2 minutes.
7. Do quick pressure release.
8. Once the lid is open, press the Sauté button and allow to simmer until the sauce thickens or evaporates.

Nutrition information: Calories per serving: 118; Carbohydrates: 16.3g; Protein:5.6 g; Fat: 5.4g; Fiber: 6.2g

Whole foods 30 Cauliflower Rice

Serves: 4
Preparation Time: 5 minutes
Cooking Time: 8 minutes

Ingredients
- 1 large head of cauliflower, cut into florets
- 2 tablespoons olive oil
- ¼ teaspoon salt
- A dash of black pepper
- Chopped cilantro for garnish

Instructions
1. Place the cauliflower florets in a food processor and pulse until grain-like. If you don't have a food processor, you can grate the cauliflower heads to achieve the same results.
2. Press the Sauté button on the Instant Pot and heat the oil.
3. Add the grated cauliflower and season with salt and pepper to taste.
4. Close the lid and press the Manual button. Adjust the cooking time to 2 minutes.
5. Do a quick pressure release to open the lid.
6. Once the lid is open, press the Sauté button and continue stirring until the liquid in the cauliflower evaporates.
7. Garnish with cilantro before serving.

Nutrition information: Calories per serving: 163; Carbohydrates: 4.4g; Protein: 11.5g; Fat: 11.2g; Fiber: 1.5g

Beef, Mushroom, And Zucchini Stir Fry

Serves: 5
Preparation Time: 5 minutes
Cooking Time: 15 minutes

Ingredients
- 1 tablespoon olive oil
- 1 onion, chopped
- 6 cloves of garlic, minced
- 1-pound beef flank steak, sliced thinly
- 1 cup fresh button mushrooms, sliced
- 6 tablespoons coconut aminos
- 5 tablespoons Chinese five-spice powder
- Salt and pepper to taste
- 1 zucchini, sliced

Instructions
1. Press the Sauté button on the Instant Pot.
2. Heat the oil and sauté the onions and garlic until fragrant.
3. Stir in the beef flank steak and continue to cook for another minute.
4. Add the mushrooms, coconut aminos, and five-spice powder. Season with salt and pepper to taste.
5. Close the lid and press the Manual button.
6. Adjust the cooking time to 10 minutes.
7. Do quick pressure release to open the lid.
8. Once the lid is open, press the Sauté button.
9. Stir in the zucchini and continue cooking for another 5 minutes or until the sauce evaporates.

Nutrition information: Calories per serving: 175; Carbohydrates:5.8 g; Protein: 20.7g; Fat: 7.4g; Fiber: 1g

Whole foods 30 Veggie Lo Mein

Serves: 4
Preparation Time: 5 minutes
Cooking Time: 6 minutes

Ingredients

- 2 tablespoons olive oil
- 5 cloves of garlic, minced
- 2-inch knob of ginger, grated
- 8 ounces of mushrooms, sliced
- ½ pound zucchini, spiralized or cut into noodle-like strips
- 1 carrot, julienned
- 1 sprig green onions, chopped
- 3 tablespoons coconut aminos
- Salt and pepper to taste
- 1 tablespoon sesame oil

Instructions

1. Press the Sauté button on the Instant Pot and heat the oil.
2. Sauté the garlic and ginger until fragrant.
3. Stir in the mushrooms for at least 2 minutes.
4. Add the zucchini, carrots and green onions.
5. Season with coconut aminos, salt, and pepper.
6. Close the lid and press the Manual button. Adjust the cooking time to 2 minutes.
7. Do quick pressure release.
8. Once the lid is open, press the Sauté button and stir in the sesame oil.
9. Serve warm.

Nutrition information: Calories per serving:288; Carbohydrates: 48.7g; Protein: 7.6g; Fat: 11g; Fiber: 7.9g

Stir Fried Sesame Chicken

Serves: 5
Preparation Time: 5 minutes
Cooking Time: 15 minutes

Ingredients

- 1 ½ pound chicken breasts, cut into strips
- 3 tablespoons coconut aminos
- Salt and pepper to taste
- ¼ cup organic and unsweetened applesauce
- 1 teaspoon red pepper, crushed
- 1 tablespoon sesame seeds, toasted

Instructions

1. Press the Sauté button on the Instant Pot and stir in the chicken breasts.
2. Continue stirring until the chicken meat turns lightly golden.
3. Add the coconut aminos, salt, pepper, and applesauce.
4. Close the lid and seal off the vent.
5. Press the Poultry button and adjust the cooking time to 9 minutes.
6. Do quick pressure release.
7. Open the lid and toss in the red pepper flakes.
8. Press the Sauté button and continue stirring until the sauce thickens.
9. Stir in the sesame seeds last.

Nutrition information: Calories per serving:255; Carbohydrates:2.8 g; Protein: 28.9g; Fat: 16.3g; Fiber: 0.6g

Indian Bell Peppers and Potato Stir Fry

Serves: 2
Preparation Time: 5 minutes
Cooking Time: 15 minutes

Ingredients

- 1 tablespoon oil
- ½ teaspoon cumin seeds
- 4 cloves of garlic, minced
- 4 potatoes, scrubbed and halved
- Salt and pepper to taste
- 5 tablespoons water
- 2 bell peppers, seeded and julienned
- Chopped cilantro for garnish

Instructions

1. Press the Sauté button on the Instant Pot.
2. Heat the oil and Add the cumin seeds until fragrant.
3. Stir in the garlic and continue stirring for another minute.
4. Stir in the potatoes. Season with salt and pepper to taste.
5. Pour in the water and close the lid.
6. Press the Manual button and adjust the cooking time to 9 minutes.
7. Do quick pressure release.
8. Once the lid is open, press the Sauté button and stir in the bell peppers. Continue stirring for another 5 minutes.
9. Garnish with cilantro before serving.

Nutrition information: Calories per serving: 83; Carbohydrates: 7.3g; Protein: 2.8g; Fat: 6.4g; Fiber:1.7 g

Broccoli and Ground Beef Stir Fry

Serves: 4
Preparation Time: 5 minutes
Cooking Time: 10 minutes

Ingredients
- 1 tablespoon olive oil
- 1-pound chicken breasts, cut into strips
- 3 cloves of garlic, minced
- 1 onion, minced
- 2 tablespoons coconut aminos
- Salt and pepper to taste
- 2 tablespoons water
- 2 heads of broccoli, cut into florets

Instructions
1. Press the Sauté button on the Instant Pot.
2. Heat the oil and Add chicken breast slices.
3. Continue stirring until the chicken turns lightly golden brown.
4. Stir in the garlic and onion until fragrant.
5. Season with coconut aminos, salt, and pepper.
6. Stir in water and Add the broccoli florets
7. Pour in the water and close the lid.
8. Press the Manual button and adjust the cooking time to 5 minutes.
9. Do quick pressure release.

Nutrition information: Calories per serving: 245; Carbohydrates: 4.6g; Protein:24.4 g; Fat:13.9 g; Fiber: 0.8g

Butternut Squash Stir Fry

Serves: 4
Preparation Time: 5 minutes
Cooking Time: 10 minutes

Ingredients

- 1 tablespoon olive oil
- 3 cloves of garlic, minced
- 1 butternut squash, seeded and sliced
- 1 tablespoon coconut aminos
- 1 tablespoon lemon juice
- 1 tablespoon water
- Salt and pepper to taste

Instructions

1. Press the Sauté button on the Instant Pot and heat the oil.
2. Sauté the garlic until fragrant.
3. Add the squash and continue cooking for 3 minutes.
4. Stir in the rest of the ingredients.
5. Close the lid and seal off the vent.
6. Press the Manual button and adjust the cooking time to 6 minutes.
7. Do a natural pressure release to open the lid.
8. Once the lid is open, press the Sauté button.
9. Cook until the liquid has reduced.

Nutrition information: Calories per serving: 152; Carbohydrates: 31.4g; Protein:2.9g; Fat: 3.7g; Fiber: 4.3g

Whole foods 30 Cashew Chicken Stir Fry

Serves: 4
Preparation Time: 5 minutes
Cooking Time: 15 minutes

Ingredients
- 2 tablespoons olive oil
- 1-pound chicken breasts, cut into bite-sized pieces
- 2 cups broccoli florets
- 1 large red bell pepper, seeded and julienned
- 1 thumb-size ginger, sliced
- 6 tablespoons coconut aminos
- Salt and pepper to taste
- 1 cup unsalted cashews, toasted
- 1 tablespoon sesame seeds

Instructions
1. Press the Sauté button on the Instant Pot.
2. Heat the oil and sauté the chicken breasts until all sides turn lightly golden.
3. Stir in the broccoli, red bell pepper, and ginger.
4. Season with coconut aminos, salt, and pepper.
5. Close the lid and seal off the vent.
6. Press the Manual button and adjust the cooking time to 10 minutes.
7. Do quick pressure release.
8. Once the lid is open, press the Sauté button and stir the cashews and sesame seeds
9. Continue stirring for another 5 minutes.

Nutrition information: Calories per serving: 660; Carbohydrates: 21.3g; Protein: 36.5g; Fat: 50.3g; Fiber: 2.7g

Sautéed Indian Butter Shrimps

Serves: 6
Preparation Time: 5 minutes
Cooking Time: 10 minutes

Ingredients
- ¼ cup coconut cream, freshly squeezed or Whole foods 30 compliant
- 2 teaspoons ground cumin
- 2 teaspoons smoked paprika
- 2 teaspoons garam masala
- 2 teaspoons fresh lime juice
- 1 teaspoon grated ginger
- 1 clove of garlic, minced
- 2 pounds of large shrimps, peeled and deveined
- Salt and pepper to taste

Instructions
1. Press the Sauté button on the Instant Pot and add the coconut cream.
2. Allow the coconut cream to simmer until reduced.
3. Add the cumin, paprika, and garam masala.
4. Stir in the lime juice, ginger, and garlic.
5. Pour in the shrimps and season with salt and pepper.
6. Close the lid and seal off the vent.
7. Press the Manual button and adjust the cooking time to 3 minutes.
8. Do quick pressure release.
9. Once the lid is open, press the Sauté button and continue stirring until the shrimps are thoroughly cooked and the sauce has reduced.

Nutrition information: Calories per serving: 60; Carbohydrates: 5.7g; Protein: 1.7g; Fat: 4g; Fiber: 1.8g

Chicken, Shrimps, And Okra Stir Fry

Serves: 8
Preparation Time: 5 minutes
Cooking Time: 10 minutes

Ingredients
- 2 tablespoons olive oil
- 1 ½ pound chicken breasts, sliced into thin strips
- 1 cup chopped onions
- 3 cloves of garlic, minced
- Salt and pepper to taste
- ½ cup tomatoes, chopped
- 1-pound okra, cut into 1-inch thick
- 1-pound medium-sized shrimps, peeled and deveined

Instructions
1. Press the Sauté button on the Instant Pot and heat the oil.
2. Add the chicken breasts, onion, and garlic. Season with salt and pepper to taste.
3. Stir until the chicken meat turns slightly golden.
4. Stir in the tomatoes, okra, and shrimps.
5. Close the lid and seal off the vent.
6. Press the Manual button and adjust the cooking time to 5 minutes.
7. Do quick pressure release.
8. Once the lid is open, press the Sauté button and continue cooking until the liquid is reduced.

Nutrition information: Calories per serving: 148; Carbohydrates: 3.2g; Protein:24.8 g; Fat: 3.2g; Fiber: 0.9g

Fried Japanese Cauliflower Rice

Serves: 6
Preparation Time: 5 minutes
Cooking Time: 20 minutes

Ingredients
- 2 cups grated cauliflower heads
- 2 tablespoons sesame oil
- 1 large onion, chopped
- 3 cloves of garlic, minced
- 1 cup leftover meat (if any)
- 2 tablespoons coconut aminos
- Salt and pepper to taste
- 3 eggs, beaten
- 1 tablespoon sesame seeds
- sliced green onions for garnish

Instructions
1. Place a trivet in the Instant Pot and pour a cup of water over.
2. Place the cauliflower in a heat-proof bowl and place in the middle of the trivet.
3. Close the lid and press the Steam button. Adjust the cooking time to 10 minutes.
4. Do quick pressure release. Set the steamed cauliflower aside and discard the liquid and remove the trivet.
5. Press the Sauté button and heat the sesame oil. Sauté the onion and garlic until fragrant.
6. Add the leftover meat and steamed grated cauliflower.
7. Season with salt and pepper to taste.
8. Add the eggs and continue stirring for another 6 minutes.
9. Garnish with sesame seeds and green onions once done.

Nutrition information: Calories per serving: 132; Carbohydrates: 13.8g; Protein: 6.7g; Fat: 13.2g; Fiber: 4.7g

Stir Fried Pork with Onions

Serves: 4
Preparation Time: 5 minutes
Cooking Time: 15 minutes

Ingredients
- 4 boneless pork loin chops, cut into strips
- 1 tablespoon coconut aminos
- ½ cup grated apple
- 2 large onions, sliced
- Salt and pepper to taste

Instructions
1. Press the Sauté button on the Instant Pot and stir in the pork strips.
2. Stir until the meat turns slightly golden or has rendered its fat.
3. Pour in the coconut aminos, grated apples, and onions.
4. Season with salt and pepper to taste.
5. Close the lid and seal off the vent.
6. Press the Manual button and adjust the cooking time to 10 minutes.
7. Do quick pressure release.
8. Once the lid is open, press the Sauté button and continue cooking until the sauce has thickened and the onions caramelized.

Nutrition information: Calories per serving:214; Carbohydrates: 10.4g; Protein: 25.1g; Fat: 19.2g; Fiber: 6.3g

Leftover Sautéed Chicken with Applesauce

Serves: 5
Preparation Time: 5 minutes
Cooking Time: 10 minutes

Ingredients
- 2 tablespoons olive oil
- 3 cloves of garlic, minced
- 1 onion, chopped
- 1-pound leftover chicken, cut into strips
- 1 cup applesauce, organic and unsweetened
- ¼ cup coconut aminos
- Salt and pepper to taste
- 1 star anise
- 2 bay leaves

Instructions
1. Press the Sauté button on the Instant Pot.
2. Heat the oil and sauté the garlic and onion until fragrant.
3. Stir in the chicken and the rest of the ingredients.
4. Continue stirring and simmering for 6 minutes.
5. Serve warm.

Nutrition information: Calories per serving: 215; Carbohydrates: 6.1g; Protein: 23.6g; Fat: 12.8g; Fiber: 2.1g

Sautéed Garlic Chicken Strips

Serves: 6
Preparation Time: 5 minutes
Cooking Time: 15 minutes

Ingredients
- 1 tablespoon olive oil
- 1 ½ pounds chicken breasts, cut into strips
- 4 cloves of garlic, chopped
- 1 onion, chopped
- 1 tablespoon fresh ginger, sliced
- 2 tablespoons coconut aminos
- Salt and pepper to taste
- 1 stalk green onions, chopped

Instructions
1. Press the Sauté button on the Instant Pot and heat the oil.
2. Stir in the chicken breasts, garlic, and onion until the chicken turns lightly golden.
3. Stir in the ginger, coconut aminos, salt, and pepper.
4. Close the lid and press the Poultry button.
5. Adjust the cooking time to 6 minutes.
6. Do a quick pressure release to open the lid.
7. Once the lid is open, press the Sauté button and Add the green onions. Cook for another 3 minutes.

Nutrition information: Calories per serving:217; Carbohydrates: 2.8g; Protein: 21.7g; Fat: 15.4g; Fiber: 0.7g

Stir-Fried Garlic Shrimps

Serves: 6
Preparation Time: 5 minutes
Cooking Time: 10 minutes

Ingredients
- 3 tablespoons olive oil
- 1 tablespoon ghee or clarified butter
- 1 garlic bulb, minced
- 1 onion, chopped
- 1 bay leaf
- 2 pounds of shrimps, peeled and deveined
- Salt and pepper to taste

Instructions
1. Press the Sauté button and heat the olive oil and ghee.
2. Add the garlic and onions until fragrant.
3. Stir in the rest of the ingredients.
4. Continue stirring for a minute.
5. Close the lid but do not seal off the vent. Cover for 3 minutes.
6. Open the lid and allow to simmer until the sauce has reduced.

Nutrition information: Calories per serving: 196; Carbohydrates:0.7 g; Protein:19.7 g; Fat: 23.2g; Fiber: 0.2g

Stir-Fried Vegetables

Serves: 3
Preparation Time: 5 minutes
Cooking Time: 6 minutes

Ingredients
- 1 tablespoon olive oil
- 1 onion, chopped
- 4 cloves of garlic, minced
- 2 carrots, peeled and julienned
- 1 zucchini, julienned
- 1 large potato, peeled and julienned
- ½ cup chopped tomatoes
- 1 teaspoon rosemary sprig
- Salt and pepper to taste

Instructions
1. Press the Sauté button and heat the oil.
2. Sauté the onion and garlic until fragrant.
3. Stir in the rest of the ingredients.
4. Close the lid and make sure that the vents are sealed.
5. Press the Manual button and adjust the cooking time to 1 minute.
6. Do quick pressure release.
7. Once the lid is open, press the Sauté button and continue stirring until the liquid has reduced.

Nutrition information: Calories per serving: 97; Carbohydrates: 10.4g; Protein: 0.5g; Fat: 4.2g; Fiber: 5.3g

Beef and Bell Pepper Stir Fry

Serves: 4
Preparation Time: 5 minutes
Cooking Time: 15 minutes

Ingredients

- 2 tablespoons olive oil
- 3 cloves of garlic, minced
- 1 onion, chopped
- 1-pound top sirloin steak, cut into strips
- ¼ cup coconut aminos
- 1 teaspoon rosemary
- 1 cup green bell pepper, seeded and julienned
- 1 cup yellow bell pepper, seeded and julienned
- 1 cup red bell pepper, seeded and julienned
- Salt and pepper to taste

Instructions

1. Press the Sauté button on the Instant Pot.
2. Sauté the garlic and onion until fragrant.
3. Add the sirloin steak and season with coconut aminos and rosemary.
4. Close the lid and seal off the vent.
5. Press the Manual button and adjust the cooking time to 10 minutes.
6. Do natural pressure release.
7. Once the lid is open, press the Sauté button and stir in the rest of the ingredients.
8. Season with salt and pepper to taste.

Nutrition information: Calories per serving: 241; Carbohydrates: 10.5g; Protein: 20.6g; Fat: 13.2g; Fiber: 5.8g

Ginger-Veggie Stir Fry

Serves: 4
Preparation Time: 5 minutes
Cooking Time: 5 minutes

Ingredients
- 1 tablespoon oil
- 3 cloves of garlic, minced
- 1 onion, chopped
- 1 thumb-size ginger, sliced
- 1 teaspoon miso paste
- 1 tablespoon water
- 1 large carrots, peeled and julienned
- 1 large green bell pepper, seeded and julienned
- 1 large yellow bell pepper, seeded and julienned
- 1 large red bell pepper, seeded and julienned
- 1 zucchini, julienned
- Salt and pepper to taste

Instructions
1. Press the Sauté button on the Instant Pot.
2. Heat the oil and stir in the garlic and onions until fragrant.
3. Add the ginger slices, miso paste, and water. Melt the miso paste.
4. Add the rest of the ingredients and season with salt and pepper to taste.
5. Close the lid and seal off the vent.
6. Press the Manual button and adjust the cooking time to 2 minutes.
7. Do quick pressure release.
8. Once the lid is open, press the Sauté button and continue cooking until the sauce has reduced.

Nutrition information: Calories per serving: 102; Carbohydrates: 13.6g; Protein:0 g; Fat: 2g; Fiber: 7.6g

Chapter 5: Whole foods 30 Program Approved Casserole Recipes

Potatoes and Pepper Casserole

Serves: 6
Preparation Time: 5 minutes
Cooking Time: 15 minutes

Ingredients
- 1-pound lean ground beef
- 1 onion, chopped
- 2 cloves of garlic, minced
- 2 green peppers, chopped
- 1 cup spinach leaves, chopped
- 1 cup chopped tomatoes
- ½ cup water
- 3 large potatoes, grated
- 6 eggs, beaten
- Salt and pepper to taste

Instructions
1. Press the Sauté button and stir in the ground beef.
2. Add the onion and garlic until fragrant and until the beef has turned light brown.
3. Stir in the rest of the ingredients and mix until well combined.
4. Close the lid and press the Manual button.
5. Adjust the cooking time to 10 minutes.
6. Do natural pressure release.

Nutrition information: Calories per serving: 361; Carbohydrates: 15.2g; Protein:29.4g; Fat: 31.3g; Fiber: 9.3g

Chicken Broccoli Egg Casserole

Serves: 6
Preparation Time: 5 minutes
Cooking Time: 15 minutes

Ingredients
- 2 tablespoons ghee
- 1 yellow onion, diced
- 2 cloves of garlic, minced
- 1-pound boneless chicken breasts, sliced
- 2 cups broccoli florets
- 1 teaspoon lemon juice
- 6 eggs, beaten
- Salt and pepper to taste

Instructions
1. Press the Sauté button on the Instant Pot.
2. Heat the ghee and sauté the onion and garlic until fragrant.
3. Stir in the chicken breasts until lightly golden.
4. Stir in the broccoli florets, lemon juice, and eggs.
5. Season with salt and pepper to taste.
6. Close the lid and seal off the vent.
7. Press the Manual button and adjust the cooking time to 10 minutes.
8. Do natural pressure release.

Nutrition information: Calories per serving: 295; Carbohydrates: 8.5g; Protein: 28.3g; Fat: 32.5g; Fiber: 2.4g

Twice Baked Potato Casserole

Serves: 8
Preparation Time: 5 minutes
Cooking Time: 15 minutes

Ingredients
- 1/4 cup almonds, soaked
- ¾ cup water
- 3 tablespoons olive oil
- 3 pounds red potatoes, scrubbed and sliced
- 3 cloves of garlic, minced
- 1 teaspoon rosemary
- 1 egg, beaten
- Salt and pepper to taste
- Green onions for garnish

Instructions
1. Place the almonds in the blender and add 2 cups of water. Blend until smooth. Strain the almond and reserve the liquid. Discard the solid. Set aside.
2. Press the Sauté button on the Instant Pot and heat the olive oil.
3. Sauté the potatoes, garlic, and rosemary until fragrant.
4. Stir in the almond milk. Season with salt and pepper to taste.
5. Close the lid and seal off the vent.
6. Press the Manual button and adjust the cooking time to 10 minutes.
7. Do natural pressure release.

Nutrition information: Calories per serving: 492; Carbohydrates:35.7 g; Protein: 21.6g; Fat: 29.5g; Fiber: 2.6g

Whole foods 30 Chicken Cordon Blue Casserole

Serves: 4
Preparation Time: 5 minutes
Cooking Time: 15 minutes

Ingredients
- 1 cup cashew nuts, soaked at least 10 minutes
- 1 cup water
- 1-pound boneless chicken breasts, cut into strips
- 2 tablespoons lemon juice
- 1 teaspoon rosemary
- Salt and pepper to taste

Instructions
1. Combine the cashew nuts and water in a blender. Blend until smooth.
2. Place all ingredients in the Instant Pot.
3. Give a good stir.
4. Close the lid and seal off the vent.
5. Press the Manual button and adjust the cooking time to 15 minutes.
6. Do natural pressure release.

Nutrition information: Calories per serving: 529; Carbohydrates: 0.9g; Protein: 39.6g; Fat: 35.2g; Fiber: 0g

Chicken Pot Pie Casserole

Serves: 4
Preparation Time: 5 minutes
Cooking Time: 15 minutes

Ingredients
- 1 cup cashew nuts, soaked at least 10 minutes
- 1 cup water
- 1-pound chicken breasts, cubed
- 1 cup carrots, chopped
- 1 cup zucchini, chopped
- 2 cups water
- Salt and pepper to taste

Instructions
1. Combine the cashew nuts and water in a blender. Blend until smooth.
2. Pour into the Instant Pot including the rest of the ingredients.
3. Stir to combine.
4. Close the lid and seal off the vent.
5. Press the Manual button and adjust the cooking time to 15 minutes.
6. Do natural pressure release.

Nutrition information: Calories per serving: 298; Carbohydrates: 9.5g; Protein: 28.5g; Fat: 25.3g; Fiber: 3.1g

Whole foods 30 Chicken Enchilada Casserole

Serves: 5
Preparation Time: 5 minutes
Cooking Time: 15 minutes

Ingredients

- 1 cup cashew nuts, soaked at least 10 minutes
- 1 cup water
- 1 tablespoon lemon juice
- 3 chicken breasts, cut into strips
- 2 cups chopped tomatoes
- 1 teaspoon cumin
- 1 tablespoon chopped cilantro
- 1 ½ cups black olives
- Salt and pepper to taste
- ½ of avocado, sliced

Instructions

1. Combine the cashew nuts and water in a blender. Blend until smooth. Stir in the lemon juice. Set aside. This will be the "sour cream."
2. Place all ingredients in the Instant Pot except for the sour cream and avocado.
3. Give a good stir.
4. Close the lid and seal off the vents.
5. Press the Manual button and adjust the cooking time to 15 minutes.
6. Do natural pressure release.
7. Serve with the sour cream, avocadoes or more cilantro.

Nutrition information: Calories per serving: 529; Carbohydrates: 7.3g; Protein:39.5 g; Fat: 48.6g; Fiber: 4.6g

Chicken Gloria Casserole

Serves: 4
Preparation Time: 5 minutes
Cooking Time: 15 minutes

Ingredients
- 1 cup cashew nuts, soaked at least 10 minutes
- 1 cup water
- 1 tablespoon olive oil
- 3 cloves of garlic, minced
- 1 onion, chopped
- 1-pound chicken breasts, sliced into strips
- 1 cup fresh baby Bella mushrooms, chopped
- 1 tablespoon chopped parsley
- 2 potatoes, peeled and grated

Instructions
1. Combine the cashew nuts and water in a blender. Blend until smooth. Set aside.
2. Press the Sauté button on the Instant Pot and sate the garlic and onions until fragrant.
3. Stir in the chicken and cook until lightly golden.
4. Add the mushrooms and the rest of the ingredients.
5. Pour over the cashew cream and give a good stir.
6. Close the lid and seal off the vent.
7. Press the Manual button and adjust the cooking time to 10 minutes.
8. Do natural pressure release.

Nutrition information: Calories per serving: 481; Carbohydrates: 9.3g; Protein: 39.5g; Fat: 34.6g; Fiber: 4.2g

Alfredo Chicken Pot Pie

Serves: 8
Preparation Time: 5 minutes
Cooking Time: 10 minutes

Ingredients

- 2 cups cashew nuts, soaked at least 10 minutes
- 2 cups water
- 1 tablespoon oil
- 3 cloves of garlic, minced
- 5 cups cooked or leftover chicken, shredded
- 1 teaspoon red pepper flakes
- A dash of dried oregano
- A dash of rosemary
- Salt and pepper to taste
- Green onions for garnish

Instructions

1. Place the cashew nuts and water in a blender. Pulse until smooth.
2. Press the Sauté button on the Instant Pot.
3. Heat the oil and sauté the garlic until fragrant.
4. Stir in the chicken, red pepper flakes, oregano, and rosemary. Season with salt and pepper to taste
5. Pour in the cashew cream. Give a good stir.
6. Close the lid and seal off the vent.
7. Press the Manual button and adjust the cooking time to 5 minutes.
8. Do natural pressure release.
9. Garnish with green onions.

Nutrition information: Calories per serving: 613; Carbohydrates: 2.1g; Protein: 50.4g; Fat: 40.3g; Fiber: 0.8g

Creamy Mexican Casserole

Serves: 6
Preparation Time: 5 minutes
Cooking Time: 15 minutes

Ingredients

- 2 cups cashew nuts, soaked at least 10 minutes
- 2 cups water
- 1 tablespoon oil
- 4 cloves of garlic, minced
- 1 onion, minced
- 2 pounds lean ground beef
- 1 ½ cups chopped tomatoes
- 1 teaspoon cumin
- 1 teaspoon oregano
- 1 serrano pepper, chopped
- ½ cup cilantro, chopped
- Salt and pepper to taste

Instructions

1. Place the cashew nuts and water in a blender. Pulse until smooth. Set aside.
2. Press the Sauté button on the Instant Pot.
3. Heat the oil and sauté the garlic and onion until fragrant.
4. Add the ground beef and stir until lightly brown.
5. Stir in the chopped tomatoes and the rest of the ingredients including the cashew cream.
6. Close the lid and seal off the vent.
7. Press the Manual button and adjust the cooking time to 15 minutes.
8. Do natural pressure release.

Nutrition information: Calories per serving: 514; Carbohydrates:1.6g; Protein: 47.5g; Fat: 39.7g; Fiber: 0.7g

Sweet Potato Breakfast Casserole

Serves: 6
Preparation Time: 5 minutes
Cooking Time: 15 minutes

Ingredients
- 1 tablespoon olive oil
- 1 cup chopped onions
- 1 ½ pound sweet potatoes, peeled and cut into an inch thick
- 2 tablespoons water
- 6 large eggs, beaten
- Salt and pepper to taste
- Chopped parsley for garnish

Instructions
1. Press the Sauté button on the Instant Pot and heat the oil.
2. Stir in the onions and sauté until fragrant.
3. Arrange the sweet potato slices in the Instant Pot.
4. In a bowl, mix the water, eggs, and season with salt and pepper to taste.
5. Pour the egg mixture over the sweet potatoes.
6. Close the lid and seal off the vent.
7. Press the Manual button and adjust the cooking time to 15 minutes.
8. Do natural pressure release.
9. Garnish with chopped parsley.

Nutrition information: Calories per serving: 329; Carbohydrates:23.1g; Protein: 21.6g; Fat: 29.6g; Fiber: 12.6g

Spinach and Broccoli Breakfast Casserole

Serves: 6
Preparation Time: 5 minutes
Cooking Time: 15 minutes

Ingredients
- 1 tablespoon olive oil
- 3 cloves of garlic, minced
- 1 onion, chopped
- 2 cups broccoli florets
- 2 cups fresh baby spinach, shredded
- ½ cup almond milk, Whole foods 30 compliant
- 6 eggs, beaten
- Salt and pepper to taste

Instructions
1. Press the Sauté button on the Instant Pot.
2. Heat the oil and sauté the garlic and onion until fragrant.
3. Stir in the broccoli and spinach.
4. Pour in the milk and eggs. Season with salt and pepper to taste.
5. Close the lid and seal off the vent.
6. Press the Manual button and adjust the cooking time to 10 minutes.
7. Do natural pressure release.

Nutrition information: Calories per serving: 238; Carbohydrates: 6.9g; Protein: 25.1g; Fat: 20.8g; Fiber: 2.7g

Instant Pot Squash Casserole

Serves: 9
Preparation Time: 5 minutes
Cooking Time: 10 minutes

Ingredients

- 2 cups cashew nuts, soaked at least 10 minutes
- 2 cups water
- 1 tablespoon olive oil
- 1 onion chopped
- 9 cups sliced yellow summer squash
- 1 tablespoon lemon juice
- Salt and pepper to taste

Instructions

1. Place the cashew nuts and water in the blender. Pulse until smooth. Set aside.
2. Press the Sauté button on the Instant Pot and heat the oil.
3. Sauté the onion until fragrant.
4. Arrange the summer squash and Spread the cashew nuts on top.
5. Stir in the lemon juice and season with salt and pepper to taste.
6. Close the lid and seal off the vent.
7. Press the Manual button and adjust the cooking time to 10 minutes.
8. Do natural pressure release.

Nutrition information: Calories per serving: 320; Carbohydrates:10.5 g; Protein: 2.1g; Fat: 28.6g; Fiber:4.8g

Beef, Mushroom, And Egg Casserole

Serves: 10
Preparation Time: 5 minutes
Cooking Time: 20 minutes

Ingredients

- 1 tablespoon olive oil
- 3 cloves of garlic, minced
- 1 onion, chopped
- 1-pound lean ground beef
- 1 cup mushrooms, chopped
- 1 teaspoon sage
- 1 teaspoon rosemary
- ½ cup spinach, chopped finely
- 6 eggs, beaten
- Salt and pepper to taste

Instructions

1. Press the Sauté button on the Instant Pot.
2. Heat the oil and sauté the garlic and onion until fragrant.
3. Add the ground beef and cook until fragrant.
4. Stir in the mushrooms, sage, rosemary, and spinach.
5. Pour in the eggs and season with salt and pepper to taste.
6. Close the lid and seal off the vent.
7. Press the Manual button and adjust the cooking time to 15 minutes.
8. Do natural pressure release.

Nutrition information: Calories per serving: 301; Carbohydrates: 5.8g; Protein: 29.8g; Fat: 27.4g; Fiber: 1.7g

Herbed Turkey Casserole

Serves: 3
Preparation Time: 5 minutes
Cooking Time: 15 minutes

Ingredients
- 1 tablespoon olive oil
- 3 cloves of garlic, minced
- 1 onion, chopped
- 2 cups cooked turkey meat, shredded
- 1 cauliflower head, grated
- 3 eggs, beaten
- Salt and pepper to taste

Instructions
1. Press the Sauté button on the Instant Pot.
2. Heat the oil and sauté the garlic and onion until fragrant.
3. Add the turkey meat and stir for 2 minutes.
4. Stir in the cauliflower bits.
5. Pour the eggs and season with salt and pepper to taste.
6. Close the lid and seal off the vent.
7. Press the Manual button and adjust the cooking time to 10 minutes.
8. Do natural pressure release.

Nutrition information: Calories per serving: 311; Carbohydrates:0.9g; Protein:36.3g; Fat: 28.7g; Fiber: 0.1g

Chive and Onion Egg Casserole

Serves: 6
Preparation Time: 5 minutes
Cooking Time: 15 minutes

Ingredients

- 6 eggs, beaten
- ½ cup unsweetened almond milk, Whole foods 30-compliant
- Salt and pepper to taste
- 1 tablespoon olive oil
- 1 white onion, sliced
- ½ cup chives

Instructions

1. In a mixing bowl, mix the eggs and almond milk. Season with salt and pepper to taste.
2. Press the Sauté button on the Instant Pot and heat the oil.
3. Add the white onions and sauté until wilted and fragrant.
4. Stir in the chives and pour in the egg mixture.
5. Close the lid and seal off the vent.
6. Press the Manual button and adjust the cooking time to 10 minutes.
7. Do natural pressure release.

Nutrition information: Calories per serving: 328; Carbohydrates: 1g; Protein: 25.3g; Fat: 39.6g; Fiber: 0.3g

Mediterranean Minestrone Casserole

Serves: 5
Preparation Time: 5 minutes
Cooking Time: 10 minutes

Ingredients
- 3 medium carrots, chopped
- 1 onion, chopped
- 1 teaspoon oregano
- 1 teaspoon rosemary
- 1 cup diced tomatoes
- 2 potatoes, grated
- Salt and pepper to taste
- 6 eggs, beaten

Instructions
1. Place all ingredients in the Instant Pot.
2. Give a good stir.
3. Close the lid and seal off the vent.
4. Press the Manual button and adjust the cooking time to 10 minutes.
5. Do natural pressure release.

Nutrition information: Calories per serving: 197; Carbohydrates: 12.5g; Protein: 2.4g; Fat: 15.7g; Fiber: 3.5g

Beef and Potato Casserole

Serves: 4
Preparation Time: 5 minutes
Cooking Time: 20 minutes

Ingredients
- 1 cup cashew nuts, soaked for at least ten minutes
- 1 cup water
- 1 tablespoon olive oil
- 1 onion, chopped
- 4 cloves of garlic, minced
- 1-pound lean ground beef
- A dash of rosemary
- 1 cup baby Bella mushrooms, chopped
- 1-pound potatoes, sliced thinly
- Salt and pepper to taste

Instructions
1. Combine the cashew nuts and water in a blender. Blend until smooth. Set aside. This will serve as the cream.
2. Press the Sauté button on the Instant Pot and heat the oil.
3. Sauté the onions and garlic until fragrant.
4. Stir in the ground beef and rosemary. Continue stirring until the meat has turned slightly golden.
5. Add the baby Bella mushrooms and stir.
6. Stir in the sliced tomatoes and cashew cream.
7. Season with salt and pepper to taste.
8. Close the lid and seal off the vent.
9. Press the Manual button and adjust the cooking time to 15 minutes.
10. Do natural pressure release.

Nutrition information: Calories per serving: 429; Carbohydrates: 7.5g; Protein: 32.1g; Fat: 50.3g; Fiber: 2.6g

Beef and Peppers Breakfast Casserole

Serves: 9
Preparation Time: 5 minutes
Cooking Time: 15 minutes

Ingredients

- ½ cup almond nuts, soaked for at least 10 minutes.
- 1 cup water
- 9 eggs, beaten
- 1 tablespoon olive oil
- 1 onion, chopped
- 3 cloves of garlic, minced
- 1-pound lean ground beef
- Salt and pepper to taste
- 1 large yellow bell pepper, seeded and chopped
- 1 large green bell pepper, seeded and chopped
- 1 large red bell pepper, seeded and chopped

Instructions

1. In a blender, place the almond nuts and water and pulse until smooth. Strain the mixture through a sieve and save the liquid part. Discard the solids or save it for later use.
2. In a mixing bowl, mix together the eggs and the almond liquid or milk. Set aside.
3. Press the Sauté button on the Instant Pot and heat the oil.
4. Sauté the onion and garlic until fragrant.
5. Stir in the ground beef and season with salt and pepper to taste.
6. Add the bell peppers and stir for another minute.
7. Pour in the egg mixture and season with more salt and pepper if desired.
8. Close the lid and seal off the vent.
9. Press the Manual button and adjust the cooking time to 10 minutes.
10. Do natural pressure release.

Nutrition information: Calories per serving: 418; Carbohydrates: 5.3g; Protein: 29.5g; Fat: 36.3g; Fiber: 2.4g

Mixed Vegetable Casserole

Serves: 8
Preparation Time: 5 minutes
Cooking Time: 15 minutes

Ingredients

- 1 tablespoon onion powder
- 2 tablespoons garlic powder
- 8 eggs, beaten
- Salt and pepper to taste
- 1 cup broccoli florets
- 1 carrot, peeled and chopped
- 1 cup cauliflower florets

Instructions

1. In a mixing bowl, mix together the onion powder, garlic powder, and eggs. Season with salt and pepper to taste. Mix until well combined.
2. Place the vegetables in the Instant Pot and give a good stir.
3. Pour over the egg mixture.
4. Close the lid and seal off the vent.
5. Press the Manual button and adjust the cooking time to 15 minutes.
6. Do natural pressure release.

Nutrition information: Calories per serving: 187; Carbohydrates: 10.4g; Protein: 3.2g; Fat: 24.3g; Fiber: 3.9g

Extra Basil Pesto Casserole

Serves: 3
Preparation Time: 10 minutes
Cooking Time: 10 minutes

Ingredients

- ½ cup walnuts
- ½ cup pine nuts
- 3 cloves of garlic, minced
- 5 cups fresh basil leaves
- 1 lemon, juice freshly squeezed
- 1 ½ cups extra virgin olive oil
- Salt and pepper to taste
- 6 eggs, beaten

Instructions

1. In a blender, combine the walnuts, pine nuts, garlic, 3 cups of basil leaves, lemon juice, and extra virgin olive oil. Season with salt and pepper to taste. Pulse until slightly smooth. This will be the pesto sauce. Set aside
2. Grease the inner pot of the pressure cooker with cooking spray and Add the eggs.
3. Stir in the remaining basil leaves and pesto sauce.
4. Close the lid and seal off the vent.
5. Press the Manual button and adjust the cooking time to 10 minutes.
6. Do natural pressure release.

Nutrition information: Calories per serving: 314; Carbohydrates: 3.2g; Protein:15.3g; Fat: 38.5g; Fiber: 0.9g

Italian Chicken and Vegetable Casserole

Serves: 7
Preparation Time: 5 minutes
Cooking Time: 15 minutes

Ingredients
- 1 tablespoon olive oil
- 2 cups cooked or leftover chicken, shredded
- 1 tablespoon Dijon mustard
- A dash of dried oregano
- A dash of dried thyme
- A dash of dried rosemary
- 2 medium potatoes, peeled and chopped
- 2 medium carrots, peeled and chopped
- 1 cup diced tomatoes
- 6 eggs, beaten
- Salt and pepper to taste

Instructions
1. Press the Sauté button on the Instant Pot and heat the olive oil.
2. Stir in the leftover chicken and add the Dijon mustard, oregano, thyme, and rosemary. Stir for another minute.
3. Stir in the potatoes, carrots, and tomatoes. Continue stirring for 2 minutes.
4. Pour in the eggs and season with salt and pepper to taste.
5. Close the lid and seal off the vent.
6. Press the Manual button and adjust the cooking time to 10 minutes.
7. Do natural pressure release.

Nutrition information: Calories per serving: 276; Carbohydrates:15.8 g; Protein: 24.9g; Fat: 23.6g; Fiber: 3.2g

"Baked" Fish and Veggies Casserole

Serves: 6
Preparation Time: 5 minutes
Cooking Time: 20 minutes

Ingredients
- 1 teaspoon olive oil
- 1 onion, diced
- 3 cloves of garlic, minced
- 3 cups potatoes, diced
- A dash of sage
- 1 cup water
- Juice from 1 lemon, freshly squeezed
- Salt and pepper to taste
- 2 cod fillets, sliced into strips
- 2 tablespoons balsamic vinegar

Instructions
1. Press the Sauté button on the Instant Pot and heat the oil.
2. Sauté the onion and garlic until fragrant.
3. Stir in the potatoes and sage and stir for 1 minute.
4. Add water and lemon juice.
5. Season with salt and pepper to taste.
6. Place the cod strips on top and drizzle with balsamic vinegar.
7. Close the lid and seal off the vent.
8. Press the Manual button and adjust the cooking time to 15 minutes.
9. Do natural pressure release.

Nutrition information: Calories per serving: 279; Carbohydrates: 21.7g; Protein: 15.6g; Fat: 13.2g; Fiber:3.1g

Shredded Turkey and Vegetables Casserole

Serves: 4
Preparation Time: 5 minutes
Cooking Time: 10 minutes

Ingredients

- 1 tablespoon oil
- 1 white onion, chopped
- 2 cloves of garlic, minced
- 1-pound cooked turkey meat, shredded
- A dash of rosemary
- 1 zucchini, chopped
- 1 carrot, peeled and chopped
- ½ cup water
- Salt and pepper to taste

Instructions

1. Press the Sauté button on the Instant Pot and heat the oil.
2. Sauté the onion and garlic until fragrant.
3. Add the turkey meat and stir for 1 minute. Season with rosemary.
4. Stir in the zucchini and carrots and stir for a minute.
5. Pour in the water and season with salt and pepper to taste.
6. Close the lid and seal off the vent.
7. Press the Manual button and adjust the cooking time to 6 minutes.
8. Do natural pressure release.

Nutrition information: Calories per serving: 243; Carbohydrates: 19.5g; Protein:21.7 g; Fat: 9.7g; Fiber: 2.9g

Winter Root Veggies Casserole

Serves: 6
Preparation Time: 5 minutes
Cooking Time: 20 minutes

Ingredients
- 1-pound lean ground beef
- 1 onion, diced
- 1 large baking potato, cut into ½ inch cubes
- 1 orange sweet potato, cut into ½ inch cubes
- 2 medium carrots, sliced
- 1 medium parsnips, sliced
- 1 cup chopped parsley
- Salt and pepper to taste

Instructions
1. Press the Sauté button on the Instant Pot and stir in the lean ground beef.
2. Stir until the beef has rendered some of its fat.
3. Stir in the onions until fragrant and Add the vegetables.
4. Season with salt and pepper to taste.
5. Close the lid and seal off the vent.
6. Press the Manual button and adjust the cooking time to 15 minutes under low pressure.
7. Do natural pressure release.

Nutrition information: Calories per serving: 295; Carbohydrates:19.6 g; Protein: 21.7g; Fat: 10.4g; Fiber: 4.8g

Chicken Enchilada Casserole

Serves: 10
Preparation Time: 10 minutes
Cooking Time: 25 minutes

Ingredients

- 5 pitted dates
- 3 tablespoons olive oil
- ¼ cup chili powder
- 1 cup water
- 1 cup tomato paste
- 1 teaspoon ground cumin
- 1 teaspoon dried oregano
- Salt and pepper to taste
- 2 pounds of chicken breasts, cut into strips
- 1 sweet potato, scrubbed and chopped

Instructions

1. In a blender or food processor, place the dates, olive oil, chili powder, water, tomato paste, cumin, and oregano. Season with salt and pepper to taste. Pulse until smooth. This will be the enchilada sauce.
2. On the Instant Pot, place the chicken breasts and sweet potatoes.
3. Pour over the enchilada sauce.
4. Close the lid and seal off the vent.
5. Press the Manual button and adjust the cooking time to 20 minutes.
6. Do natural pressure release.

Nutrition information: Calories per serving: 374; Carbohydrates: 22.8 g; Protein: 29.6g; Fat: 19.7g; Fiber: 2.4g

Chapter 6: Whole foods 30 Program Approved Slow-Cooked Recipes

Instant Pot Slow Cooker Turkey Chili

Serves: 6
Preparation Time: 5 minutes
Cooking Time: 8 hours

Ingredients
- 2 tablespoons olive oil
- 1-pound ground turkey
- 1 onion, chopped
- 1 green bell pepper, seeded and chopped
- 3 carrots, peeled and chopped
- 2 stalks of celery, sliced thinly
- 1 cup chopped tomatoes
- 3 poblano chilies, chopped
- ½ cup water
- 3 tablespoons chili powder
- 1 ½ teaspoons ground cumin
- Salt and pepper to taste

Instructions
1. Press the Sauté button on the Instant Pot.
2. Heat the oil and add the turkey meat and onions. Sauté until fragrant and the turkey meat has turned slightly golden.
3. Stir in the bell peppers, carrots, celery, tomatoes, and chilies.
4. Pour in water and season with chili powder, cumin, salt, and pepper.
5. Close the lid and make sure that the steam release is set to "venting".
6. Press the Slow Cooker button and adjust the cooking time to 8 hours.
7. Cook at low temperature.

Nutrition information: Calories per serving: 296; Carbohydrates: 9.9g; Protein:25.3 g; Fat: 19.5g; Fiber: 3.2g

Slow Cooker Hawaiian Kalua Pig

Serves: 8
Preparation Time: 5 minutes
Cooking Time: 12 hours and 5 minutes

Ingredients

- 1 5-pound pork shoulder, bone in
- 5 cloves of garlic, crushed and peeled
- 1 ½ tablespoons salt
- 1 cup water
- 1 cup pineapple juice, fresh

Instructions

1. Place all ingredients in the Instant Pot.
2. Close the lid and make sure that the steam release is set to "venting".
3. Press the Slow Cooker button and adjust the cooking time to 12 hours.
4. Cook at low temperature.
5. Once done, take the meat out and use forks to shred the meat.
6. Place the meat back into the Instant Pot and press the Sauté button.
7. Allow to simmer for 5 minutes

Nutrition information: Calories per serving: 341; Carbohydrates: 6.1g; Protein: 36.3g; Fat: 21.6g; Fiber: 0g

Coconut Chicken Curry

Serves: 6
Preparation Time: 5 minutes
Cooking Time: 6 hours and 5 minutes

Ingredients
- 1 tablespoon olive oil
- 2 tablespoons garam masala
- 1-inch ginger, sliced
- 2 cloves of garlic, minced
- 2 tomatoes, chopped
- 3 pounds of chicken breasts, skin and bones removed
- Salt and pepper to taste
- 1 cup water
- 2 cups coconut cream, freshly squeezed

Instructions
1. Place all ingredients except for the coconut cream in the Instant Pot.
2. Close the lid and make sure that the steam release is set to "venting".
3. Press the Slow Cooker button and adjust the cooking time to 6 hours.
4. Cook at low temperature.
5. Once done, open the lid and pour in the coconut cream.
6. Press the Sauté button and allow to simmer for 5 minutes.

Nutrition information: Calories per serving: 492; Carbohydrates: 6.7g; Protein: 58.3g; Fat: 30.7g; Fiber: 0.9g

Instant Pot Applesauce

Serves: 4
Preparation Time: 5 minutes
Cooking Time: 8 hours

Ingredients
- 6 large peeled apples, cored and sliced
- 2 cinnamon sticks
- 1 tablespoon lemon juice, freshly squeezed
- ½ cup water
- ¼ teaspoon salt

Instructions
1. Place all ingredients in the Instant Pot.
2. Close the lid and make sure that the steam release is set to "venting".
3. Press the Slow Cooker button and adjust the cooking time to 8 hours.
4. Cook at low temperature.
5. Open the lid and discard the cinnamon sticks.
6. Pour the apple mixture into a blender and pulse until smooth.

Nutrition information: Calories per serving: 144; Carbohydrates: 38.2g; Protein: 0.7g; Fat: 0.5g; Fiber: 15.7g

Slow Cooker Shredded Chicken

Serves: 4
Preparation Time: 5 minutes
Cooking Time: 8 hours and 5 minutes

Ingredients

- 2 pounds of chicken breasts, bones and skin removed
- 1 cup water
- 1 bay leaf
- Salt and pepper to taste

Instructions

1. Place all ingredients in the Instant Pot.
2. Close the lid and make sure that the steam release is set to "venting".
3. Press the Slow Cooker button and adjust the cooking time to 8 hours.
4. Cook at low temperature.
5. Once the timer beeps, open the lid and take the chicken out.
6. Shred using two forks.
7. Place the chicken back into the Instant Pot and press the Sauté button.
8. Simmer for 5 minutes.

Nutrition information: Calories per serving: 670; Carbohydrates: 0g; Protein: 68.3g; Fat: 30.1g; Fiber: 0g

Slow Cooker Meatballs

Serves: 6
Preparation Time: 15 minutes
Cooking Time: 8 hours

Ingredients

- ¼ cup parsley, chopped
- 1-pound lean ground pork
- ½ yellow onion, chopped finely
- 1 egg, beaten
- 1 clove of garlic, minced
- Salt and pepper to taste
- 2 cups chopped tomatoes
- 1 sprig of rosemary
- 3 pitted dates
- 1 bay leaf

Instructions

1. In a mixing bowl, combine the parsley, pork, onion, egg, and garlic. Season with salt and pepper to taste. If it is dry, add a few tablespoons of water if needed.
2. Form small balls of the meat mixture using your hands and place inside the greased Instant Pot.
3. In a blender, mix together the tomatoes, rosemary, and dates. Season with salt and pepper. Blend until smooth.
4. Pour the sauce carefully over the meatballs. Place the bay leaf.
5. Close the lid and make sure that the steam release is set to "venting".
6. Press the Slow Cooker button and adjust the cooking time to 8 hours.
7. Cook at low temperature.

Nutrition information: Calories per serving: 238; Carbohydrates: 10.5g; Protein: 27.2g; Fat: 28.6g; Fiber: 2.6g

Slow Cooker Caramelized Onions

Serves: 6
Preparation Time: 5 minutes
Cooking Time: 6 hours

Ingredients
- 3 tablespoons olive oil
- 3 pounds of large yellow onions, sliced
- Salt to taste

Instructions
1. Press the Sauté button on the Instant Pot and heat the olive oil.
2. Add the onions and season with salt.
3. Stir for 2 minutes until fragrant.
4. Close the lid and make sure that the steam release is set to "venting".
5. Press the Slow Cooker button and adjust the cooking time to 6 hours.
6. Cook at low temperature.

Nutrition information: Calories per serving: 160; Carbohydrates:16.4 g; Protein:1.9g; Fat: 10.3g; Fiber: 3g

Slow Cooker Chicken Adobo

Serves: 9
Preparation Time: 5 minutes
Cooking Time: 8 hours

Ingredients

- 1 whole chicken, cut into bite-sized pieces
- ½ cup lemon juice, freshly squeezed
- ½ cup coconut aminos
- 5 cloves of garlic, crushed
- 2 onions, quartered
- 1 bay leaf
- Salt and pepper to taste

Instructions

1. Place all ingredients in the Instant Pot.
2. Close the lid and make sure that the steam release is set to "venting".
3. Press the Slow Cooker button and adjust the cooking time to 8 hours.
4. Cook at low temperature.

Nutrition information: Calories per serving: 281; Carbohydrates: 1g; Protein: 39.2g; Fat: 23.4g; Fiber: 0.4g

Slow Cooker Brisket and Onions

Serves: 6
Preparation Time: 5 minutes
Cooking Time: 12 hours

Ingredients

- 1 tablespoon olive oil
- 1 ½ pounds red onions, sliced
- 3 ½ pounds beef brisket
- 6 cloves of garlic
- 1 ½ cups water
- ½ cup coconut aminos
- Salt and pepper to taste

Instructions

1. Press the Sauté button on the Instant Pot.
2. Heat the oil and stir in the red onions until fragrant.
3. Pour in the rest of the ingredients.
4. Close the lid and make sure that the steam release is set to "venting".
5. Press the Slow Cooker button and adjust the cooking time to 12 hours.
6. Cook at low temperature.

Nutrition information: Calories per serving: 379; Carbohydrates:0.2g; Protein: 30.4g; Fat: 23.6g; Fiber: 0g

Slow Cooker Pork Carnitas

Serves: 18
Preparation Time: 5 minutes
Cooking Time: 12 hours

Ingredients
- 1 6-pound pork butt, bone in
- 2 tablespoons salt
- 1 tablespoon ground black pepper
- 1 tablespoon ground cumin
- 2 teaspoons cinnamon
- 8 cloves of garlic, chopped
- 1 cup chopped tomatoes
- 4 chipotle peppers, chopped

Instructions
1. Place all ingredients in the Instant Pot.
2. Close the lid and make sure that the steam release is set to "venting".
3. Press the Slow Cooker button and adjust the cooking time to 12 hours.
4. Cook at low temperature.

Nutrition information: Calories per serving: 342; Carbohydrates: 3.4g; Protein: 24.6g; Fat: 25g; Fiber: 0.9g

Coconut Curry Pork

Serves: 8
Preparation Time: 5 minutes
Cooking Time: 12 hours

Ingredients

- 1 3-pounds pork butt, bone in
- 2 teaspoons salt
- ½ teaspoon ground black pepper
- 4 curry leaves
- 2 cups coconut milk, freshly squeezed or Whole foods 30 compliant
- ½ pound potatoes, cubed
- ¼ cup chopped cilantro

Instructions

1. Place all ingredients in the Instant Pot.
2. Close the lid and make sure that the steam release is set to "venting".
3. Press the Slow Cooker button and adjust the cooking time to 12 hours.
4. Cook at low temperature.

Nutrition information: Calories per serving: 537; Carbohydrates: 25.1g; Protein: 32.5g; Fat: 34.8g; Fiber: 3g

Slow Cooker Barbacoa Beef

Serves: 16
Preparation Time: 5 minutes
Cooking Time: 12 hours

Ingredients
- 3 dried jalapeno peppers, chopped
- 1 bunch fresh cilantro, chopped
- 1 red onion, chopped
- 1 bulb of garlic, minced
- 1 teaspoon ground cloves
- 7 pounds of briskets
- 6 cups water
- 5 bay leaves
- Salt and pepper to taste

Instructions
1. Place all ingredients in the Instant Pot.
2. Close the lid and make sure that the steam release is set to "venting".
3. Press the Slow Cooker button and adjust the cooking time to 12 hours.
4. Cook at low temperature.

Nutrition information: Calories per serving: 328; Carbohydrates: 4.5g; Protein: 18.8g; Fat: 21.8g; Fiber: 2.2g

Korean Short Ribs

Serves: 7
Preparation Time: 5 minutes
Cooking Time: 12 hours

Ingredients
- 6 pounds of beef short ribs
- 1 medium pear, peeled, cored and chopped
- ½ cup coconut aminos
- 6 cloves of garlic, minced
- 1-piece ginger, sliced
- 1 tablespoon coconut vinegar
- 1 cup water
- 4 tablespoons chili paste
- 2 tablespoons sesame oil
- Salt and pepper to taste

Instructions
1. Place all ingredients in the Instant Pot.
2. Close the lid and make sure that the steam release is set to "venting".
3. Press the Slow Cooker button and adjust the cooking time to 12 hours.
4. Cook at low temperature.
5. Garnish with scallions and toasted sesame seeds.

Nutrition information: Calories per serving: 578; Carbohydrates:0.9g; Protein: 52.4g; Fat: 32.9g; Fiber: 0.1g

Slow Cooker Chicken Tikka Masala

Serves: 6
Preparation Time: 5 minutes
Cooking Time: 8 hours and 10 minutes

Ingredients
- 1 tablespoon ghee
- ½ onion, chopped
- 3 cloves of garlic, chopped
- 1 ½ pounds chicken thighs, bones and skin removed
- Salt and pepper to taste
- 1 teaspoon grated ginger
- 1 teaspoon ground coriander
- 1 teaspoon cumin
- ½ teaspoon garam masala
- ¼ teaspoon cardamom powder
- 1 can chopped tomatoes
- 1 cup water
- 2 cups cauliflower florets
- ½ cup coconut milk, freshly squeezed
- ¼ cup fresh cilantro, for serving

Instructions
1. Press the Sauté button on the Instant Pot and heat the ghee.
2. Sauté the onion and garlic until fragrant.
3. Add the chicken thighs and stir for 2 minutes.
4. Season with salt and pepper and the spices (ginger, coriander, cumin, garam masala, and cardamom).
5. Stir for 2 more minutes.
6. Pour in the tomatoes and water.
7. Close the lid and make sure that the steam release is set to "venting".
8. Press the Slow Cooker button and adjust the cooking time to 8 hours.
9. Cook at low temperature.
10. Halfway through the cooking time, Add the cauliflower florets and coconut milk. Close the lid.
11. Once done, garnish with cilantro.

Nutrition information: Calories per serving: 226; Carbohydrates: 9g; Protein:26 g; Fat:10g; Fiber: 2.5g

Citrus-Braised Chicken in Slow Cooker

Serves: 4
Preparation Time: 5 minutes
Cooking Time: 8 hours and 5 minutes

Ingredients
- 1 tablespoon olive oil
- 3 cloves of garlic, minced
- 5 pounds of whole chicken, cut into bite-sized pieces
- Salt and pepper to taste
- 2 medium oranges, peeled and quartered
- 1 cup water
- Salt and pepper to taste

Instructions
1. Press the Sauté button on the Instant Pot and heat the oil.
2. Sauté the garlic until fragrant and Add the chicken meat.
3. Continue stirring for 3 minutes until lightly fragrant.
4. Add the rest of the ingredients.
5. Close the lid and make sure that the steam release is set to "venting".
6. Press the Slow Cooker button and adjust the cooking time to 8 hours.
7. Cook at low temperature.

Nutrition information: Calories per serving: 527; Carbohydrates: 16.6g; Protein: 60.2g; Fat: 28.7g; Fiber: 1.6g

Instant Pot Whole foods 30 Chili

Serves: 5
Preparation Time: 5 minutes
Cooking Time: 8 hours and 5 minutes

Ingredients

- 1 ½ pound lean ground beef
- 1 onion, diced
- 4 cloves of garlic, minced
- 1 cup chopped tomatoes
- 2 tablespoons chili powder
- 1 yellow bell pepper, seeded and chopped
- 1 orange bell pepper, seeded and chopped
- 1 red bell pepper, seeded and chopped
- 1 tablespoon cumin
- 2 cups water
- Salt and pepper to taste

Instructions

1. Press the Sauté button on the Instant Pot and heat the ground beef.
2. Stir until the beef starts to render some fat.
3. Add the rest of the ingredients.
4. Close the lid and make sure that the steam release is set to "venting".
5. Press the Slow Cooker button and adjust the cooking time to 8 hours.
6. Cook at low temperature.

Nutrition information: Calories per serving: 196; Carbohydrates: 4.6g; Protein: 15.4g; Fat: 10.2g; Fiber: 1.3g

Slow Cooker Chinese Ribs

Serves: 3
Preparation Time: 5 minutes
Cooking Time: 12 hours

Ingredients
- 1 rack baby back ribs
- 3 star anise
- 3 bay leaves
- 2 tablespoons Chinese five-spice powder
- ¼ cup fish sauce (Red Boat's)
- ¼ cup coconut aminos
- 1 cup water
- 1 teaspoon black peppercorns
- Salt to taste

Instructions
1. Place all ingredients in the Instant Pot.
2. Close the lid and make sure that the steam release is set to "venting".
3. Press the Slow Cooker button and adjust the cooking time to 12 hours.
4. Cook at low temperature.

Nutrition information: Calories per serving: 296; Carbohydrates: 0.7g; Protein: 29.3g; Fat: 18.6g; Fiber: 0 g

Slow Cooker Beef Stew

Serves: 4
Preparation Time: 5 minutes
Cooking Time: 10 hours

Ingredients

- 2 pounds of chuck steak, cut into strips
- 3 cloves of garlic, minced
- 2 onions, sliced
- 12 white mushrooms, sliced
- 2 stalks of celery, chopped
- 2 bay leaves
- 1 ½ cup water
- 1 tablespoon fish sauce (Red Boat's)
- 3 tablespoons organic tomato paste
- Salt and pepper to taste

Instructions

1. Place all ingredients in the Instant Pot and give a good stir.
2. Close the lid and make sure that the steam release is set to "venting".
3. Press the Slow Cooker button and adjust the cooking time to 10 hours.
4. Cook at low temperature.

Nutrition information: Calories per serving:433; Carbohydrates: 12.8g; Protein: 39.2g; Fat:21.2 g; Fiber: 6.7g

Mississippi Pot Roast

Serves: 10
Preparation Time: 5 minutes
Cooking Time: 12 hours

Ingredients

- 2 pounds marbled chuck roasts, cut into cubes
- ¾ cup water
- 1 teaspoon onion powder
- 1 teaspoon garlic powder
- 1 teaspoon dill weed
- 1 teaspoon dried chives
- 1 tablespoon olive oil
- 5 pepperoncini peppers, chopped
- Salt and pepper to taste

Instructions

1. Place all ingredients in the Instant Pot.
2. Close the lid and make sure that the steam release is set to "venting".
3. Press the Slow Cooker button and adjust the cooking time to 12 hours.
4. Cook at low temperature.

Nutrition information: Calories per serving: 145; Carbohydrates: 11g; Protein: 7.9g; Fat: 5.1g; Fiber: 0g

Slow Cooker All-American Pot Roast

Serves: 4
Preparation Time: 5 minutes
Cooking Time: 12 hours

Ingredients

- 3 pounds of chuck roast, sliced into chunks
- 4 cloves of garlic, minced
- 2 onions, chopped
- 1 cup water
- 1 tablespoon fish sauce (Red Boat's)
- 1 tablespoon olive oil
- A dash of rosemary
- A dash of thyme
- 2 bay leaves
- 2 carrots, chopped
- 4 potatoes, quartered
- Salt and pepper to taste

Instructions

1. Place all ingredients in the Instant Pot.
2. Close the lid and make sure that the steam release is set to "venting".
3. Press the Slow Cooker button and adjust the cooking time to 12 hours.
4. Cook at low temperature.

Nutrition information: Calories per serving: 472; Carbohydrates:19.6g; Protein: 32.5g; Fat: 21.7g; Fiber: 104g

Simple Short Ribs

Serves: 5
Preparation Time: 5 minutes
Cooking Time: 10 hours

Ingredients
- 3 pounds of beef short ribs
- 1 onion, sliced
- 3 stalks of celery, diced
- 3 carrots, diced
- 1 cup water
- ¼ cup lemon juice, freshly squeezed
- 1 teaspoon paprika
- ½ teaspoon chili powder
- ½ teaspoon dry mustard
- Salt and pepper to taste

Instructions
1. Place all ingredients in the Instant Pot.
2. Close the lid and make sure that the steam release is set to "venting".
3. Press the Slow Cooker button and adjust the cooking time to 10 hours.
4. Cook at low temperature.

Nutrition information: Calories per serving: 492; Carbohydrates: 8.4g; Protein: 53.4g; Fat: 23.5g; Fiber: 2.8g

Slow Cooker Whole foods 30 Sloppy Joes

Serves: 4
Preparation Time: 5 minutes
Cooking Time: 12 hours

Ingredients
- 1 tablespoon olive oil
- 1 ½ pounds lean ground beef
- 1 onion, diced
- 1 green bell pepper, diced
- 1 red bell pepper, diced
- 3 cloves of garlic, minced
- 1 tablespoon coconut aminos
- 1 teaspoon Dijon mustard
- 1 tablespoon pitted dates, chopped
- ½ cup water
- Salt and pepper to taste

Instructions
1. Press the Sauté button on the Instant Pot.
2. Heat the oil and stir in the ground beef and onions until fragrant and slightly rendered.
3. Stir in the rest of the ingredients.
4. Close the lid and make sure that the steam release is set to "venting".
5. Press the Slow Cooker button and adjust the cooking time to 12 hours.
6. Cook at low temperature.

Nutrition information: Calories per serving: 562; Carbohydrates: 10.5g; Protein: 42.6 g; Fat: 28.5g; Fiber: 13g

Slow Cooker Lamb Leg Roast

Serves: 12
Preparation Time: 5 minutes
Cooking Time: 12 hours

Ingredients
- 1 tablespoon ghee
- 6 cloves of garlic, crushed
- 3 sprigs of rosemary
- 3 sprigs of thyme
- 1/3 cup stone ground mustard
- 4 pounds of boneless lamb leg roast
- 2 cups water
- Salt and pepper to taste

Instructions
1. Press the Sauté button on the Instant Pot.
2. Heat the oil and sauté the garlic, rosemary, and thyme. Stir in the mustard.
3. Add the lamb leg and sear all sides for 2 to 3 minutes each.
4. Pour in the rest of the ingredients.
5. Close the lid and make sure that the steam release is set to "venting".
6. Press the Slow Cooker button and adjust the cooking time to 12 hours.
7. Cook at low temperature.

Nutrition information: Calories per serving: 378; Carbohydrates: 1g; Protein: 39.4g; Fat: 17.5g; Fiber: 0.3g

Slow Cooker BBQ Chicken Wings

Serves: 9
Preparation Time: 5 minutes
Cooking Time: 8 hours

Ingredients

- 2 pounds of chicken breasts, bones removed
- ½ cup organic tomato paste
- 1/3 cup water
- ¼ cup coconut aminos
- 2 tablespoons date paste or finely chopped dates
- 2 tablespoons raw apple cider vinegar
- 1 teaspoon onion powder
- ½ teaspoon garlic powder
- ½ teaspoon smoked paprika

Instructions

1. Place all ingredients in the Instant Pot.
2. Close the lid and make sure that the steam release is set to "venting".
3. Press the Slow Cooker button and adjust the cooking time to 8 hours.
4. Cook at low temperature.
5. Once cooked, use forks to shred the chicken.

Nutrition information: Calories per serving: 401; Carbohydrates: 10.6g; Protein: 29.6g; Fat:7.6 g; Fiber: 3.1g

Made in the USA
Middletown, DE
19 April 2019